SEW SUBVERSIVE
Down & Dirty DIY for the Fabulous Fashionista

Melissa Rannels ☆ Melissa Alvarado ☆ Hope Meng

Illustrated by Hope Meng & 3+Co.
Photographs by Matthew Carden

The Taunton Press

The Taunton Press
Inspiration for hands-on living®

The Taunton Press, Inc., 63 South Main Street, PO Box 5506, Newtown, CT 06470-5506
e-mail: tp@taunton.com

Editor: Pam Hoenig
Jacket/Cover design: 3+Co.
Interior design: 3+Co.
Layout: 3+Co.
Illustrators: Hope Meng and 3+Co.
Photographer: Matthew Carden

Library of Congress Cataloging-in-Publication Data
Alvarado, Melissa.
  Sew subversive : down and dirty DIY for the fabulous fashionista /
Melissa Alvarado, Melissa Rannels, and Hope Meng ; Illustrated by Hope Meng.
     p. cm.
  Includes bibliographical references and index.
  ISBN-13: 978-1-56158-809-1 (alk. paper)
  ISBN-10: 1-56158-809-1 (alk. paper)
  1. Girls' clothing. 2. Clothing and dress--Remaking. I. Rannels, Melissa. II. Meng,
Hope. III. Title.
  TT562.A49 2006
  646.4'04--dc22

                    2006001502

Printed in China
10 9 8 7 6 5 4 3 2 1

Dedicated to the original lovers of yard sales, regulars at remnant bins, and masters of seam rippers, our own scalding hot moms: Carolyn, Kathy, and Wendy

Many effusive thanks to our fabulous editor, Pam, the ever-delightful Katie, and the rest of the good people of The Taunton Press that made Sew Subversive a reality. Thanks to The Boys (Albabe, Jacob, and Jeremy) who stood by our sides and supported our venture into authorhood, and to the rest of our friends and families that believe in us and all our crazy ideas. Thank you to the locations where we had fun photo shoots in fantastic spaces: 111 Minna Street Gallery, Britex Fabrics, Michael Ferris Gibson's house, and Silver Lucy's Attic Studio Space. Super props to our friends for rockin' it as our ridiculously good looking models: Chri, Erika, Fati, Grace, Hannah, Jayne, LA Cool K, Lucid, Lucy, Silver Lucy, Special K, & Tin-Tin, with delightful hair by Edo Salon and gorgeous makeup by Carolyn Forlee. Muchas gracias to the designers that participated in the "I heart NY refashion challenge" (Anaconda, Asarum, Faeriedust Creations, Fati, Kamileon, & Leticia Huerta) and Helena for sharing her garment remake with us. Danke to Marcy Tilton for her support in spreading the modern sewing circle. And merci beaucoup to Matt at 350 Degrees Photography for being a delight and snapping such snazzy shots!

And finally, a special über thanks to our peeps at Stitch Lounge. You make our community happen and put a sparkle in the space and a spring in our step! Our urban sewing lounge exists because of your willingness to share your creativity and passion.

xoxo
Two Melissas and a Hope

CONTENTS

MAKING IT YOUR OWN: EMBELLISHING AND CUSTOMIZING CLOTHES 80

REFASHIONING: THE NEXT LIFE OF YOUR OLD CLOTHES 118

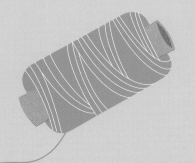

INTRODUCTION

FASHION: SUBVERTED

You've seen her. She's the cute hipster on the bus, rocking out to her pink iPod℠, wearing a halter top she made from a wool sweater. She's the adorable girl at the coffee shop talking on her cell phone, wearing the skirt with a patch on it from her favorite indie band. She is the confidently cool girl driving down the street on a vintage Vespa® scooter, armed with a clever tote bag made from an old concert T-shirt. Who is she, and why can't we stop staring at her? She's a lady with individual style. A lass with unique panache. A girl with a little somethin' different. She's the explorer who conquered the fashion world by doing things on her terms. She could be you!

We—the self-taught seamsters, the lovers of yard sales, the regulars at remnant bins, the masters of seam rippers, the conquistadoras of mass-produced fashion, the scalding-hot mamas of *Sew Subversive*—want to help you find your inner *je ne sais quoi*, cut it up, sew it, and turn it into a fashion statement of your own. We want you to share in the joy of personalized clothing that brings a smile to your face—clothing that screams your name to anyone who will listen.

Fashion is a frame for our identity: This makes differentiation in fashion not just a desire, but a must. We may have found comfort wearing what everyone else did in grade school, but not today. (It nearly kills us to see our outfit cheating on us with another woman! That naughty outfit—running off with someone else when we wore it so well!) Part of our mission with this book is to help you see that fashion choices extend beyond the ones dictated to you by retailers. In *Sew Subversive*, we will show you how to use sewing as a tool to subvert conventional fashion and put your individual mark on the clothes you wear. It won't be long before you're basking in the pride that comes from being asked, "Wow, where did you get that shirt?" and answering, "I made it."

YOU CAN DO IT YOURSELF!

Don't know your bobbin from your feed dog? Never fear! We are the first to admit there is much to learn about the intricacies of sewing, but realistically, you don't need to know it all to get started. We will break it down for you, demystifying the concepts of sewing and the sewing machine. We'll demonstrate that with some basic sewing knowledge, a dollop of design sensibility, and a little bit of imagination, finding your own fashion is easy. A bunch of our

projects don't even need a sewing machine—just get some scissors (no running!) or an iron and you'll be on the road to hot action. Caution: While you aren't required to have a machine, be prepared that you may well be scheming to get yourself one when you see how fun and easy machine sewing can be!

    Sew Subversive is chock full of fashion-subverting sewing projects that bring out the true potential in your clothes. You'll learn how to add cool designs and doodads to the clothes in your wardrobe to make a *you* statement, alter the fit of your "almost-perfect" clothes, and give a face-lift (or even a whole new life) to the clothes in your giveaway bag.

YOU CAN DO IT TOGETHER!

Sewing is often viewed as a solo sport, but it's even better as a team event. The three of us have known each other since childhood and share a love of sewing and creating. We have spent many fun evenings bonding in a modern version of the sewing circle, where inspiration and ideas flow freely. But the lack of space for large sewing rooms in the typical San Francisco home made it difficult to widen our sewing circle without the benefit of a large, centralized, commercial space. Thus, the idea of our venture—Stitch, an urban sewing lounge—was born.

Stitch Lounge is designed for creating and collaborating. It has a well-stocked sewing studio (complete with a coffee machine) where you can rent machines and specialty equipment by the hour or enjoy a sewing class or private lesson with a local designer. If you want to get inspired, Stitch has an Inspiration Section devoted to all kinds of crafty ideas and gently loved clothing with tons of potential, yearning to be turned into your favorite outfit. Stitch also supports the community of up-and-coming San Francisco designers with a boutique exhibiting their wares. The energy at Stitch is all about learning, camaraderie, and simply having fun sewing together. Every day at Stitch Lounge we see the benefits of sewing in a community!

Students getting their learn on at Stitch Lounge.

So, when you finish this book (or perhaps even just get halfway through), start callin', e-mailin', and textin' your creative, not-afraid-to-make-mistakes, fun, and unique crafty friends. Get together and start sewin' subversively. Use the skills and tools we lay out to build your own crafty community that encourages creation, inspiration, and self-expression by using what you already have and making your things on your terms!

HAND-SEWING BASICS

Now that you know why you should sew, you need to learn *how* to sew subversively. This chapter is all about getting the subversive home sewer started. While we are not traditionally trained seamsters, we have learned a lot from our moms, our friends, and, of course, good old trial and error. So let's get started!

First off, sewing doesn't have to involve an electrical appliance. Hand sewing is a good (and safe) place to learn the fundamentals. Like stapling papers, sewing is simply connecting pieces of fabric together with thread (we actually don't recommend staples in place of stitches). Whether closing a hole in your jeans or making a ball gown, it's all sewing.

Hand sewing is time-consuming if you're making an entire garment, but it's a great choice for fixing things and getting into awkward spots where a machine won't fit. One of the best things about hand sewing is the equipment you'll need: With a needle, some thread, and scissors (in a pinch you can get away with nail clippers), you're good to go. Our moms would like us to tell you not to use your teeth to cut thread. You might have to do it in a jam, but it will make them sad. You know how moms can be. So please use scissors.

You can find a variety of hand-sewing needles at your local sewing or fabric store, or sometimes even in a drugstore. Needles usually come in a variety pack, with different lengths and sizes of eyeholes. One pack will do you just fine.

THREADING YOUR NEEDLE

Grab a needle and some thread (start with about one arm's length, slightly less than a yard). If the end of your thread is a little frayed, snip it off. Nothing is more frustrating than trying to stick a ragged end of thread into a needle. The sewing world is full of different suggestions about how to easily thread the eye of a needle. We just moisten one end (with your tongue or a little water), then stick it through the eye and pull it until the two ends of the thread are even (you're essentially folding your thread in half). Holding the doubled threads together as one, tie a knot in the end. Tie another knot on top of the first for good measure. You're now sew-worthy.

If you have a particularly hard time with thread-ing, try a needle threader, which can usually be found in a basic sewing kit at the drugstore, as well as at fabric stores. It is a flexible metal loop that you stick through the eye of the needle. Put the thread in the loop, pull the loop back through the eye, and your needle is threaded!

THE STITCHES

To sew subversively (for the projects that don't require a machine), you need only three stitches:

☆ Running stitch
☆ Blanket stitch
☆ Barely visible stitch

Running stitch

This is a simple over-under-over-under stitch used for your run-of-the-mill sewing purposes. The super-duper easiest way to do a straight running stitch is to stab the needle down into the fabric (taking care not to poke your finger), pull it all the way through until it catches on the knot at the end of the thread, stab it back up through the fabric about a pinkie fingernail's

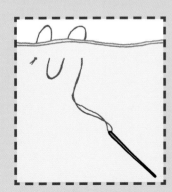

width away (make sure not to stab your pinkie while doing this—there is nothing subversive about bleeding all over your project), and pull it through tightly. Keep this over-under stabbing going until you've gotten to the end of where you need to sew.

Blanket stitch

The blanket stitch is a cute way to bind the cut edges of a piece of fabric to give them a finished look and to keep them from fraying. It can also be used to attach appliqués and patches. It is basically a finishing stitch that is meant to be visible (unlike a running stitch, which, while visible, shouldn't call attention to itself). As such, the blanket stitch is a great opportunity to use contrasting thread for a funky finish.

Stick your needle from the back of your fabric

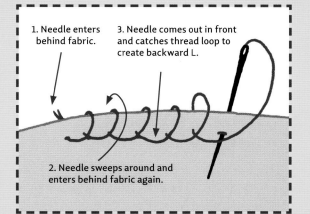

1. Needle enters behind fabric.

3. Needle comes out in front and catches thread loop to create backward L.

2. Needle sweeps around and enters behind fabric again.

to the front, about ¼ inch from the edge you want to finish, then loop over the edge of the fabric and poke your needle through ¼ inch to the right of your previous stitch. Use the tip of your needle to grab the loop you just made and create the corner of a backward L. Your stitches need to be loose so you can have that extra thread to make the L. Repeat all the way around the length of your edge. The distance in from the edge and the width of your stitches are up to you, but a good standard is to start them ¼ inch from the edge and space them ¼ inch apart.

Barely visible stitch

The barely visible stitch, as we like to call it, is used when you don't want the thread to show on the front of your garment (for example, to hem

Barely visible stitch (front)

Barely visible stitch (back)

those fabulous, too-long pants you got on sale). You will essentially be making a running stitch; the only difference is that the part of the stitch that is showing on the outside of the garment will be very, very short (imagine the shortest stitch you could possibly make that still moves forward). The stitch made in the back or inside of the garment will take up the slack and be much longer.

There are tons of other stitches out there, but these three will get you through most basic sewing projects. We'll come back to them in the upcoming projects, so make a mental note, or tag this page if you're into that sort of thing.

OK, on to business. Let's see what we can do with our three stitches.

MENDING A RIP IN A SEAM

The Scenario: You're sitting in your morning staff meeting looking down at your pants, trying to hide the fact that you're nodding off, when you notice that your inner thigh seam has sprung a leak.

Before Sewing Subversively: "How long has that been there? I hope no one noticed! Now I have to buy new pants!"

Now That You Sew Subversively: "How long has that been there? I hope no one noticed! Good thing I have my sewing kit in my purse. I'll mend it during lunch."

Come twelve o'clock, you hit the ladies' room and get to work.

1. Close the stall door. Lock it. Take off your pants. Turn them inside out and find the hole in the seam.

2. Thread your needle with some thread that closely matches the color of your pants. If you don't have an exact match, choose one that's darker than your fabric—it won't show as much as a lighter-colored thread. Remember to tie a double knot at the end of the doubled-up thread.

3. Insert the threaded needle ¼ inch to the right of one end of the hole, along the seam line.

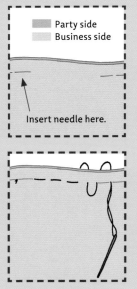

Party side
Business side

Insert needle here.

4. Make short running stitches along the seam line until you reach ¼ inch past the other side of the hole.

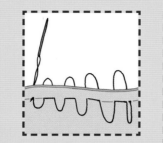

5. Repeat this line of stitches back and forth a couple of times until you feel the hole is securely mended.

6. Pick up a small amount of fabric with your needle (figure 1), make a slip knot with the thread by inserting the needle back through the loop (figure 2), and pull it tight with the needle. Repeat this knot four times.

7. Cut the thread close to the fabric, turn your pants right-side out, put them on, and get back to work.

Figure 1   Figure 2

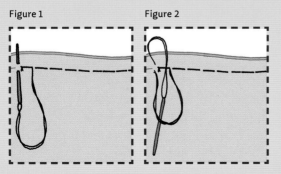

SEWING A BUTTON BACK ON

The Scenario: **You're in a rush to get to class. As you are putting on your favorite "smart" pants, your button flies off!**

Before Sewing Subversively: **"Now I have to change and find time to take these pants to the dry cleaner to get them fixed! And I'm going to be late!"**

Now That You Sew Subversively: **"OK, take a deep breath and relax. I'll sew that button back on in a flash as soon as I can sneak off to the ladies' room."**

In order to sew on a button, you'll need a needle, thread, and a safety pin.

Come break time, you hit the ladies' room and get to work.

1. Close the stall door. Lock it. Take off your pants and have a seat (we suggest using a paper seat cover).

2. Thread your needle with thread that closely matches the color of your button. Don't forget to tie a double knot at the end of the doubled-up thread.

3. Find the spot where the button was attached. You should see small holes in the fabric where it was previously attached, but if not, decide where the button should go (its placement should match the buttonhole).

4. Pin the outside of your pants with a safety pin so the center of the pin crosses the spot you

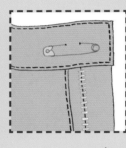

want to sew. The pin will act as a spacer to ensure that you have some thread space between the button and your pants. (This comes in handy when you eat too much Thai food for lunch and need a little extra give.)

5. Insert the needle (from the inside of your pants toward the outside) where the button was sewn on before. As the needle passes through the fabric, insert it through one of the holes in the button and pull it all the way through. Push the button against the fabric. Now insert the needle down through one of the other holes in the button and back into the fabric. You're sewing *around* the inserted leg of the pin. Your needle should be inside your pants now.

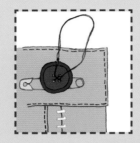

6. Do this about 10 times, alternating coming in and out of the different holes in the button, ending up with a thread X in the center. You'll want to do this enough times that your button feels secure.

7. Finish with the needle inside your pants, make some slip knots (see step 6 on page 11), and cut your thread close to the fabric.

8. Button up and get back to it!

PATCHING THINGS UP

The Scenario: It's late Sunday morning. You're just about to change out of your pj's into your favorite jeans, have a quick cup of joe, and meet up with some friends for brunch. Oh, no! Your jeans have a hole in a most inappropriate place!

Before Sewing Subversively: "Now I have to get a new pair of jeans and break them in for three months! And what will I wear today?"

Now That You Sew Subversively: "OK, take

a deep breath and relax. I'll sew a patch on as soon as I get a sip of coffee in me."

In order to sew on a patch, you'll need, well, a patch (one that is larger than the hole), safety pins, a needle, and some thread. Your patch can be a patch you picked up at your local sewing shop, an old Girl Scout badge, a name badge from your dad's old bowling shirt, or even that little piece of fabric with the cool pattern that you never knew what to do with. Whatever you have lying around should work, as long as it's sturdy and won't fray. Now, have another sip of coffee and get started.

1. Put your jeans on. Place the patch over the hole and make sure it covers the whole thing.
2. Pin the patch into place with safety pins. Too much coffee before this step could turn it into a dangerous operation. Please use caution. Take the jeans off. (Or you can take them off first, pin the patch into place, then try the jeans on again to make sure the patch fully covers. Then take them off again.)
3. Thread your needle with thread that closely matches the color of the edge of your patch (or it could contrast—whatever you prefer),

tying the obligatory double knot at the end of the doubled-up thread.

4. Pick a corner of the patch to start from and poke your needle from the inside out. You can use a running stitch or a blanket stitch all the way around the edges of the patch.
5. Finish with the needle inside your jeans, make some slip knots (see step 6 on page 11), and cut your thread close to the fabric.
6. Put yourself back into your jeans, zip up, finish your coffee, and get to brunch!

This patching technique applies to appliqués and decorative patches as well as those that actually cover a hole. Once you've done it up right, no one will even suspect that your patch is actually serving a purpose besides looking cute!

HEM IT UP

The Scenario: **You found the perfect pants that make you look hot and bootylicious, but they are 2 inches too long.**

Before Sewing Subversively: **"Now I have to get them altered and won't be able to wear them this weekend!"**

Now That You Sew Subversively: "I'll hem those babies up in a jiffy and be good to go on Friday night!"

To hem your pants, you'll need safety pins, a needle, and some thread. The thread should match the color of the pants as closely as possible. Traditionally schooled seamsters would use a fancy blind stitch here, but we're going to let you in on a shortcut using our barely visible stitch. It might not be as fancy, but it will get you out on the town in your pants. And who's going to look at your hems when your pants look so good everywhere else? Keep in mind, if you have a really fancy pair of lined pants, you may want to take them to a tailor. But our quick-and-dirty method should work for most standard britches.

1. Put your pants on inside out. Yes, inside out—trust us. Fold your cuffs up to the desired length. Stand up straight and check the length in a full-length mirror. (If you don't have a full-length mirror, get an opinion from a friend you trust, or stand on a chair before the bathroom mirror—just don't fall off.)

2. Pin them with safety pins to hold the fold securely in place. It's easiest to have a friend help with this, but you can do it by yourself. If you have more than a couple of inches to hem up, we recommend you cut off the excess material until your pants are the desired length plus 1 inch. To do this, after cuffing, take the pants off and pin all the way around with safety pins about 1 inch above your desired cuff length. Carefully cut off the excess amount above the safety pins. Always visually check to make sure you are removing the same length from both legs by comparing the leg inseams and then comparing the length of the cuff *before* you cut. (Our moms would like to remind you to "measure twice, cut once.") If you make a mistake, just remember—pants that look great on top can also become capris or shorts that look equally great! Just keep on hemming!

3. Double-check that each of the legs is the same length by comparing the length of the inseam (the distance from the crotch to the ankle fold) on each leg side by side. Better yet, put them on again for one last length check. Adjust your cuffs and re-pin as necessary. Leave them inside out.

4. Assuming the material of your pants is iron-safe, now is a good time to iron each cuff right where you want it to be. This will make your job infinitely easier, but it isn't mandatory.

5. Thread your needle and tie a double knot in the end of the doubled-up thread.

6. Start on the inside of one of the ankles at the inside seam. You will be using the barely visible stitch. Stab your needle through both layers of the pants about ¼ inch below the

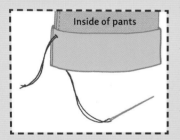

top of the material. Remember that the thread knot will be on the inside of your pants once you turn them right-side out. (We wouldn't really use maroon thread to hem lime green pants. The whole point of a barely visible stitch is that you don't see the stitch—we just illustrated it this way so you could see things more clearly.)

7. Peek on the other side and watch while you stab the needle back into your pants. (You'll

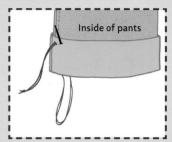

be looking at the side that will be visible once you wear your pants the correct way.) Make the itty-bittiest stitch you can, just past where your needle came out, without entering in the exact same place. This sounds harder than it actually is.

8. Now the needle is back on the side where you started. Stab into both layers of fabric about ½ inch past where you just pulled the needle through. Make another itty-bitty stitch. By now, you should be making the connection that the messy threads are going to

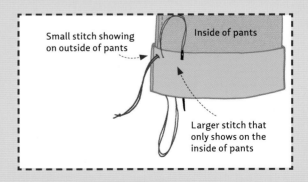

Small stitch showing on outside of pants

Larger stitch that only shows on the inside of pants

REAL SIMPLE HEMMING

★ Hand-sewing hems can take a long time and, let's be honest, be a big pain. We make hot clothes in order to wear them, not to spend our lives sitting around sewing them. Busy folks that we are, we have uncovered some quick alternatives to hand-sewing a hem.

★ Leave the edges raw. Simple enough! Trim your edges so they are even and, hey, you're done! The only caveat to this method is that if you are using a woven fabric (see "Fabric 101" on page 58 for more information), the unfinished edges will fray and unravel. But don't worry! There is a solution. You can either cut the edges with pinking shears (see page 53) or read on for the scoop on Fray Check™ and other time-saving luxuries. If you are cutting a knit (stretchy) fabric, you have nothing to worry about. Knit fabrics are constructed in such a way that the edges do not unravel. Your only concern with knits is aesthetics: If you don't like the look of a raw edge, then you'll need to hem it. Personally, we like that deconstructed look, but the choice is yours.

★ Fray Check (also sold under names like Fray-Stop™ or Fray Block™ or other such monikers that indicate its job of making sure your fabric doesn't fray). This magical liquid binds your edges so they—you guessed it—don't fray. Just dot it on the edges of your woven fabric and let it dry. (It dries mostly clear, but it can darken your material a little, so always test a small, inconspicuous spot to make sure you are OK with the results.) It is similar to using clear nail polish on a panty-hose run.

★ Fusibles. Another thread-free option for adhering two fabrics together is fusibles, which are materials that get sticky (on one or both sides) when you iron them, then fuse to whatever they're touching. (Whatever they're touching can also mean your iron or ironing board, so use them with caution!) Stitch Witchery® and Steam-A-Seam® are two of our favorites. Basically, you put the fusible between the two fabrics you want to connect, and iron! The fusible will make them stick together as if glued.

• Most fusibles are relatively permanent. Some have an adhesive side (like a sticker) that you can attach to one fabric for easy placement and movement. Others will remain unsticky until ironed and, once ironed, become permanent. Remember, you never want to iron directly onto a fusible because it will gunk up your iron. Your best insurance is to read the manufacturer's instructions in order to get the full scoop and disclaimers.

be on the inside of your cuffs, with tiny, barely visible stitches facing the rest of the world. (We'll keep that messy side our little secret!)

9. Keep going until you make it all the way around the leg hole.

10. Once you've been around the leg once, make some slip knots (see step 6 on page 11) and cut the thread close to the fabric.

11. Repeat steps 6 through 10 on the other leg.

12. Turn your pants right-side out and remove the safety pins. Try them on again and admire your smokin' hot self in the mirror!

MOVING ON UP TO THE MACHINE

Hand sewing is an effective way of tackling small projects and can also be used on bigger ventures if you've got some patience. But once you've mastered the needle and thread, it is time to consider the sewing machine as a faster means of getting those great ideas out on fabric. Read on to find out more about what could become your best crafting friend—the sewing machine.

YOU & YOUR MACHINE

Hand sewing gets the job done, but it requires your hands and eyes to make strong, even stitches—a task that can be a challenge to do consistently, even for advanced seamsters. Once you're comfortable with hand sewing and ready to complete your projects more efficiently or take on more ambitious projects, it's time to meet Mr. Sewing Machine.

A seamster's warning before we start: Don't start thinking that this machine is the sewing version of a microwave—push a button and all the work's done. Sewing on a machine requires the same patience and diligence that hand sewing does. The main benefit is that, with a sewing machine, you get strong, consistent stitches that don't take nearly as much time to complete.

Using different top and bobbin
threads adds an interesting color
twist to your garment.

HOW A SEWING MACHINE WORKS

Unlike hand sewing, a sewing machine doesn't do the over-under-over-under thread action you learned in the last chapter. Instead, it loops two threads together, one coming from the spool of thread that sits on top of the machine and the other feeding from the bobbin underneath. With the proper tension on these threads, the loops form a chain that sits perfectly within the thickness of the fabric. In other words, if you could see a cross section of the fabric, the chain would lie inside the fabric.

KNOW THY MACHINE

Understanding the anatomy of your machine is paramount to your sewing success. You must know how to operate your machine to get your sew on. And knowing your machine will help prevent frustrating errors and allow you to troubleshoot them when they do happen (and believe us, they will, no matter your skill level!). Just keep in mind that making mistakes is part of getting to know the machine. It's like your first fight with a new flame—though the argument may be upsetting, you'll learn more about each other and how you work together as a couple.

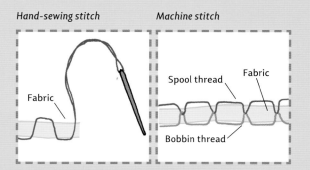

Hand-sewing stitch / *Machine stitch*

Fabric

Spool thread / Fabric / Bobbin thread

1. BOBBIN CASE (BOBBIN INSIDE NOT SHOWN)
2. FEED DOG
3. PRESSER FOOT
4. NEEDLE
5. THREAD GUIDE
6. THREAD GUIDE
7. STITCH PATTERN SELECTOR
8. THREAD UPTAKE LEVER
9. THREAD GUIDE
10. TENSION METER
11. BOBBIN WINDER THREAD GUIDE
12. STICH PATTERNS
13. THREAD SPOOL PIN
14. BOBBIN WINDER
15. HAND WHEEL
16. STITCH WIDTH SELECTOR
17. FOOT PEDAL
18. POWER SWITCH
19. STITCH LENGTH SELECTOR
20. REVERSE STITCH CONTROL

Power switch (18)

First things first! Make sure your machine is plugged in and turn the power switch to the "on" position. You will know the machine is on when the light above the needle is on (assuming the bulb isn't dead) and the needle starts to move when you press the foot pedal (17).

Needle (4)

The needle is one of the most important yet least discussed parts of the machine. Machine needles are different from hand needles because the hole is on the same end as the point. The top of the needle, called the shank, is opposite the needle point; the shank is what gets inserted into the machine. The part of the needle below the shank is called the shaft. Some needles, called universal needles, have a flat side on the shank (this indicates the back of the needle), while others are completely round. The front of a machine needle has a long groove along the shaft and the back has a cutaway piece right around the hole, known as the scarf. Most machine needles are oriented on the machine with the front of the needle facing you, but every so often you will see a machine

with the front of the needle facing your left hand.

Before you get started, get yourself a variety of needle sizes. To be sure you are getting the correct type of needle, take the needle out of your machine (see "Changing the Needle" on page 44 for how to remove the needle) and bring it to the fabric store. Most machines take universal needles. You can purchase a variety pack of universal needles that includes several different sizes. The needle size refers to the width of the shaft—a larger needle size (like 14, 16, or 18) will have a wider shaft, will be stronger, and will make a bigger hole in your fabric. Try starting with a size 11. Anything larger than a size 11 is used for

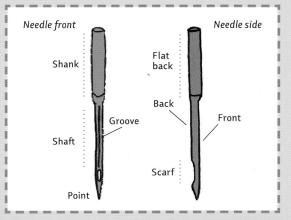

23

thick fabrics like heavy canvas (size 14) or faux fur (size 16 to 18); anything smaller is meant for use with delicate fabrics like silk or satin (size 8 to 9).

Bobbin & bobbin case (1)

A bobbin is a little metal spool that you wind thread around. The bobbin contains the second source of thread in the chain (the first coming from the spool atop your machine). Depending on

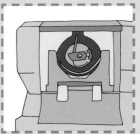
Front-loading bobbin

the model of your machine, the bobbin case can be external or internal, and it is loaded either in the top or in the area just below the needle. The bobbin and the bobbin case (which the bobbin is set in before being placed in a front-loading machine) are specific to the make and model of your machine and should not be interchanged with other types. When you go to purchase bobbins, make sure to bring one from

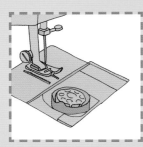
Top-loading bobbin

your sewing machine to ensure you're getting the correct one. (Other bobbins might look like they fit in your machine, but don't be fooled! Using the wrong bobbin will cause unnecessary frustration.)

Bobbin winder (14)

This is a peg that holds and spins the bobbin while simultaneously filling it with thread. Some machines have the bobbin winder on the side, but for most machines, it's on the top. This part of the machine will make a lot more sense after we go over "Filling the Bobbin" (page 38).

Bobbin winder thread guide (11)

Like the tension meter (10), this part of the machine helps create tension in the spool thread when you're filling your bobbin. It is very important to run the thread from the spool through the bobbin thread guide before it goes to the bobbin winder. If you run your thread directly from the spool to the bobbin winder, the thread will wind unevenly, which will cause problems when you are sewing. Setting this up can vary a lot from one brand of machine to another, so be sure to consult your machine's manual.

Thread spool pin (13)

The thread spool pin is the tall metal or plastic pin that sits on top of or behind the top right side of the machine. It holds the spool of thread so the machine can feed thread through to the needle. The thread spool pin can be vertical or horizontal; if your pin sits horizontally, your machine will typically come with a little cap to put at the end of the spool so it doesn't fly off when you're sewing.

Thread guides (5, 6, 9)

When threading the machine, you need to direct the thread to certain spots so that it runs correctly through the system. Some machines have only one thread guide, while others have more. They are usually located on the top and front of the machine, and it is important to use *all* of them. Consult your machine's manual to make sure you are threading it correctly. Once you've practiced

on several different machines, you'll be able to sit down and figure out any threading system.

Thread uptake lever (8)

This lever moves up and down as the needle moves up and down and stitches are made. You can see this happen if you turn the hand wheel (15) toward you. (The same thing happens when

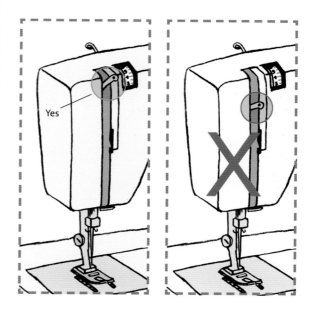

Yes

Always stop sewing with the thread uptake lever in the "up" position.

you press the foot pedal (17); it just happens a lot faster.) When the thread uptake lever is in the top position, the machine has finished making a stitch; therefore, it is important always to finish stitching with the lever in the top position. If it does not stop there automatically, you need to turn the hand wheel to move the lever to the top. Always turn the hand wheel *toward* you—if you turn it backward, you risk getting the spool thread caught on something below the needle plate. Having the uptake lever in the top position also means the needle has been pulled out of the fabric entirely, allowing you to remove your project.

Tension meter (10)

(Deep breath): OK, now for the Tension Talk.

Tension is the single most wonderful and frustrating thing about sewing. It is key to your success and enjoyment of sewing. In fact, the entire machine is set up to create a system of tension in your thread. In order to make nice, even stitches, the thread needs to feed through the machine consistently. If the thread runs loosely, the stitches will not be uniform. The tension meter, a dial that controls how tightly two metal plates inside

TROUBLESHOOTING TENSION

If your stitches are not lying flat (for instance, if the fabric is "curling" in one direction or another), then your tension is off. To fix this, try the following:

1. Sew your stitch with the tension setting you were using when the stitches were not lying flat.
2. Turn the tension meter dial one setting up (for example, if you were using a 5 setting, turn it to 6). Sew about 1 inch of stitches.
3. Now, turn the tension meter dial one setting down from the original setting (in this case, turn it to 4). Sew about 1 inch of stitches.
4. Compare the stitches and see which ones (from step 2 or from step 3) look more correct—that is, even and flat. Continue making stitches at each setting in the "correct" direction of the dial until the stitch looks perfectly even and flat. (For instance, if the stitches started looking flatter when you turned the dial to 6, turn it to 7 and sew, 8 and sew, 9 and sew, etc.)

the machine are squeezed together, controls the tension in the thread, which is fed between them. This, in turn, affects how quickly or slowly the thread is fed through the rest of the machine.

The tension meter on your machine will most likely have settings that run from 0 to 9. A well-calibrated machine will usually sew best with a tension setting between 3 and 5. Of course, this differs on every machine, and with different types of thread and fabric. Some machines will indicate the average tension setting by marking off certain numbers on the dial. Check your machine and manual for the ideal setting for your model. If you have to sew at the extreme ends of the dial, like 0 or 9 (and you are not working on a specialty fabric like silk or faux fur), it is probably time to take your machine in for a tune-up.

Stitch length selector (19)

Adjusting the stitch length changes the distance between your stitches. A shorter length makes for more secure stitches, but they are also more diffi-cult to remove if you mess up. The longest length setting is known as a basting stitch and is used when you know you are going to take the stitch

out later. It is only used to temporarily hold two pieces of fabric together, so we don't recommend a super-long stitch for your sewing projects.

As a beginner, you probably want to start with a mid-range stitch length setting (for instance, if your stitch length setting goes from 0 to 5, use 2.5 or 3). Feel

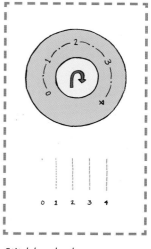

Stitch length selector

free to change the setting and play around a little so you know what the stitches at different settings look like. You will rarely use a 0 stitch length (the needle will sew in place). Stitch length applies to both straight and zigzag stitches.

Stitch width selector (16)

Adjusting the stitch width changes how wide, from left to right, your stitches will be. A straight stitch is actually a zigzag stitch with zero width. Many machines will have the straight and zigzag stitch on the same stitch pattern setting, so you

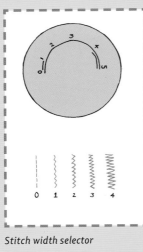

Stitch width selector

indicate a straight stitch by setting the stitch width to zero.

Stitch pattern selector (7)

This function changes the style of stitch that the machine makes when you press the foot pedal (17). Although there are many patterns to experiment with (for example, there are stitches that look like little diamonds, or ovals), all you really need for basic sewing projects are the straight and zigzag stitches. Again, on some machines, the straight stitch and zigzag stitch pattern share the same stitch pattern selection. On other machines, the straight and zigzag stitches will each have their own settings.

Reverse stitch control (20)

The reverse button (or lever, depending on your machine) is used to sew backward. In order to use it, you hold down this control while depressing the foot pedal (17). When you release the button or lever, the machine will automatically disengage and begin sewing forward again.

Presser foot (3)

The presser foot holds the fabric down against the feed dog (2) so you can make nice, even stitches. It is either up or down, and the position is usually controlled by a lever at the back of the machine (though sometimes it's on the right side of the needle). You *must* have the presser foot down when you press the foot pedal! You'll find out pretty quickly why this is so important—sew with the presser foot up and you'll get a jumbled mess of thread. Different kinds of feet (zipper, buttonhole, and so on) are used for different sewing techniques. Your machine will usually come with several, and the manual will help you figure out what to do with each of them.

Feed dog (2)

It's not just an item on your daily to-do list, it's a vital part of your sewing machine! The feed dog consists of textured metal plates (they look like bars with little teeth) located below the presser foot. They move back and forth at a consistent rate when you press the foot pedal, and they propel the fabric away from you as you sew. That's right, the machine moves the fabric for you; you don't push or pull it through! Don't worry, your hands do have a job: They must guide the fabric as it enters the sewing area so it doesn't swivel around the needle.

Foot pedal (17)

This is the gas pedal of the sewing machine. You depress the foot pedal in order to engage the gears and motor of the machine. Some machines are faster than others, and some models have a more sensitive foot pedal. The first time you use the sewing machine, it may feel like a bucking bronco, but with patience, you will learn to find the sweet spot—the amount of pressure on the foot pedal that makes the machine sew at the rate you are most comfortable with. (When you first start out, try sewing barefoot— you will be more sensitive to the amount of pressure you are exerting and it will help you find that sweet spot.)

Hand wheel (15)

The hand wheel performs the same function as the foot pedal, only much more slowly. You should always turn the hand wheel toward you, though at times you may need to jiggle it back and forth if the needle gets stuck underneath the sewing area.

So now you have a general idea of the parts of the machine, but quite possibly are more confused than when you started. Don't worry if it hasn't all sunk in just yet. The goal in introducing the parts of the machine first is to equip you with a language with which to discuss the how-to's of basic sewing. Once you start working with the machine, it will all become clear. We promise!

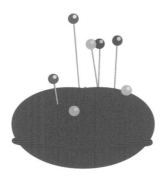

**Finding your sewing mate:
Is he the one for you?**

FINDING THE PERFECT MATE

Picking the sewing machine that's right for you is a personal decision, based on your budget and sewing needs. Sewing machines are like *beaus*—each brand and model of sewing machine has its own personality, and it is important to "date" different types of machines before settling down with The One (or at least The First One).

Particular makes of sewing machines behave and react in different ways. The knobs and controls can look different, the speed and strength can be different, and the way they respond to your touch can be different, too. Your relationship with your machine will be just like any other—sometimes life together is pure bliss; other times you'll want to curl up with a bottle of cabernet and pretend as though your mate doesn't exist. (We hope you function somewhere a little closer to bliss most of the time.) Go ahead—sew your wild oats and find the machine that suits you best!

Start your search for the perfect mate by going on several machine blind dates. Try a range of machines and brands in the store (or even go to several stores). This shouldn't be a problem, as long as you don't sit down and try to sew an entire outfit in the showroom. Check out the basics of

the machine and see what turns you on.

There are simple machines that cover the basics and fancier models that can be linked to your computer and practically run themselves—but, not surprisingly, these come with a bling-bling price tag. Before you go searching for the perfect machine, set a budget and sensibly evaluate your sewing needs. Whether you have a closet full of half-completed craft projects (yes, your honor, guilty as charged!) or you're the next Martha Stewart, evaluate your needs realistically. The last thing you want to do is buy an expensive machine that will end up being an overpriced paperweight.

While you're hunting for the perfect mate, don't forget older sewing machines. While they might

be heavy and a pain to lug around, well-cared-for older (often all-metal) machines can give the new, plastic machines a serious run for their money. You may hit paydirt in your mom's attic or at a flea market or yard sale.

THREE TIPS TO FINDING THE PERFECT SEWING MATE

1. *Get set up by a friend!* Ask your friends currently in sewing relationships what they like and dislike about their machine and ask (nicely) if you can, perhaps, take their machine out for a night on the town. (You promise to treat him nicely and have him home at a decent hour.) If you don't have any friends with sewing machines, try dating online. Unfortunately, there is no sewing-machine_match.com (at least not yet!). However, the Internet does have more reviews and opinions than you can shake a stick at. Don't trust everything little thing you read, but do try to get a sense of the pros and cons of different machines, based on your sewing level and budget.

2. *Use your local resources to go out and mingle!* If your city has a sewing lounge or studio where you can use different machines, try it out. While you might have to pay to use the machines, no one is going to try to sell you anything. A good sewing studio will have experts on hand who can teach you how the machines work and talk candidly about the strengths and weaknesses of various brands. Always try before you buy!

3. *Beware the eager sewing salesperson.* Before you enter a store, set a budget and stick to it. You'll always go home happy.

EVALUATING THE QUALITIES OF YOUR MACHINE MATE

What follows is a 101 of machine features, from our favorite must-haves to those we can live happily without:

★ *The ability to make straight and zigzag stitches.* This is a **must** for versatility (see "Straight vs. Zigzag Stitching" on page 42).

★ *Stitch width selector.* Some machines come with the zigzag width on the stitch pattern selector (i.e., you choose a wider zigzag on the pattern selector rather than on the stitch width dial). For more versatility, get a machine that has a separate stitch width dial. This allows you to choose in-between settings like 2.5 or 4.25 instead of locking you into a width of 2, 3, or 4.

★ *Removable flat bed attachment.* Newer machines come with an attachment that you can remove to create a free-arm sewing machine (i.e., a sewing machine with a narrower base below the needle so you can sew in tight areas, like around sleeves or necklines). This is pretty important if you plan to make clothes.

★ *A vertical spool thread pin.* We are always losing the little cap that holds the horizontal spool on the pin. Keeping track of a removable part of the machine is a recipe for frustration.

★ *Metal parts.* A lot of modern machines come with plastic internal parts, which are cheaper but break more often. Call us old-fashioned, but we prefer machines like Mom used to have—with metal gears and stuff.

★ *The ability to raise the presser foot higher than ¹/₄ inch.* Some machines allow you to raise the presser foot higher than usual. This is not a deal breaker, but it is an especially helpful feature when you are working with thicker fabrics.

★ *Buttonhole pattern selection.* Though not necessary, this is a seriously drool-worthy feature. It allows you to make a buttonhole with a flip of the pattern selector. Many post-1990 sewing machines come with this. Some machines even change to the appropriate stitch width and length when you have the buttonhole pattern selected.

★ *Ability to control the pressure on the presser foot.* Some machines come with a gauge that allows you to control the amount of pressure the presser foot is placing on the fabric. This allows you to tighten the pressure if you are working with a delicate material like silk, or loosen it if you are working with a bulky fabric like faux fur.

★ *Needle-changing knob (instead of a screw).* We hate having to find that pesky screwdriver every time we need to replace the needle (see "Changing the Needle" on page 44).

★ *Adjustable needle positioning.* This lets you adjust the needle to the left or right of center if you want to move the needle around a bulky object (for example, the teeth on a zipper). Some machines come with different presser foot attachments that allow you to get around those bulky areas, but it's awfully nice to have the option of moving the needle out of the way.

★ *Easy Thread System.* Some machines instruct you to thread the machine the correct way with very obvious numbers or arrows. We are ambivalent about this feature because once you read "Threading the Machine" (page 37), you won't need Easy Thread!

★ *A variety of different stitch patterns.* The majority of your stitches as a beginning seamster are going to be straight or zigzag, but it's nice to have a selection of different patterns if you think you are going to be doing any decorative stitching.

★ *Thread cutter.* Some machines come with a blade mounted somewhere near the needle that you can use to cut your thread when you're done sewing. We love our thread snips, so we really don't use the blade.

★ *Adjustable speed control.* We like one speed: fast. But we recognize that some people (especially beginners) are intimidated by higher speeds. This feature allows you to grow into your machine and move the speed up when you're good and ready.

★ *Needle up/down button.* OK, we'll admit that we love this fancy feature. With the push of a button, you can move the needle up or down. But you're paying the price for this feature—it usually only comes on the more expensive machines. The hand wheel is the good old-fashioned way to do the same thing.

★ *Digital displays.* We are generally skeptical of any sort of fancy digital feature—it's expensive, and it's one more thing that can go wrong.

★ *Drop feed.* This function allows you to drop the feed dog if you want to do free-form

stitching like embroidery or darning. You won't need this for any of our projects.

★ *Drop-in automatic bobbin loading.* It's important to learn how to load your bobbin the old-fashioned way—by hand. It ensures that nothing will go wrong during loading and means you don't have to relearn the skill if you use a machine without this feature.

You may have noticed that we aren't drawn to the bells and whistles that come with a lot of expensive machines. We are not opposed to technology —we just don't think you need to spend your money on those extra features when you could invest in a simpler machine and use the cash to buy more fabric (or to download your favorite tunes to rock out to while sewing). Always keep in mind that choosing a machine is as personal as choosing a new mate—only you can decide which features you can and can't live without.

LEARNING TO USE YOUR MACHINE

There are a variety of ways to learn how to use your machine. If you buy a new machine, you're guaranteed to have a user's manual. If your used machine's previous owner kept the manual, then you're in luck as well. If you're out of luck on the manual front, you can try to order one online from the manufacturer's website. If you have the manual and some patience, you can sit down and start making your way through it. But don't just read the manual. Sewing is a hands-on activity (if this comes as a surprise to you, you may want to consider a different hobby), and it is important to teach your hands to work in tandem with your eyes and feet. Follow the instructions with test pieces of fabric (a stiff, woven fabric like denim is great to start with) to really feel and experience what the manual is saying.

If patience and a manual are not your style, find someone to teach you—a freelance seamster or sewing teacher who will walk you through the workings of your particular machine for a nominal fee. Ask the folks at your fabric or sewing machine store for a recommendation.

If you want a classroom-type setting, you can find sewing classes for all levels in most cities. If there's nothing in the phone book, again, ask at your fabric or sewing machine store—they should be able to direct you to classes in your town. Other places to look are community colleges and fashion design schools.

Now that you know about the parts of the machine and what they do, it's time to get it up and running.

THREADING THE MACHINE

As we said in our Tension Talk on page 26, it's vital to be exact when threading the machine. Although different makes of sewing machines are threaded slightly differently, once you thread a few, you'll be able to sit down at any machine and figure out where the thread goes *before* it gets to the needle.

In our example, the thread starts from the spool (placed on the spool pin) on top of the machine. It is then strung around a thread guide, down through the tension plates, (which usually hide inside the machine next to the tension meter), back up and through the thread uptake lever, and down again through two thread guides. Finally, it is inserted through the needle. It sounds complicated, so let's simplify.

Thread guides aside for the moment (since they vary by manufacturer), the thread goes through the tension plates (making it the correct tightness), then through the thread uptake (which pulls the thread off the spool), and finally through the needle (you can figure this one out). Say it three times: tension plates, thread uptake, and needle. Remember this sequence and you should be able to thread any machine in this

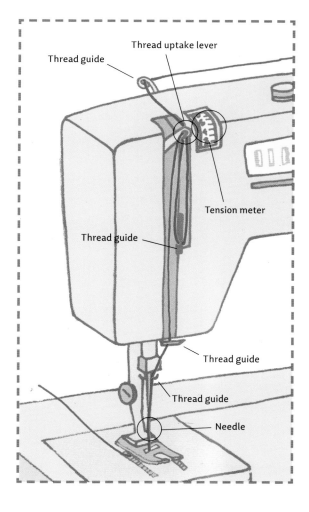

Thread guide

Thread uptake lever

Tension meter

Thread guide

Thread guide

Thread guide

Needle

universe. Your first time threading a machine will feel as complicated as surgery, but after a few tries, it'll become second nature.

FILLING THE BOBBIN

The first thing to do before you fill your bobbin is to disengage the needle (this mechanism is often called the "clutch") so it won't move up and down when you press the foot pedal. When you're filling the bobbin, you run a big risk of hurting yourself or the machine if the needle is still engaged and running up and down. Different machines have different methods of clutch release, so consult your manual.

The three primary methods are:

1. Turning a smaller wheel inside the hand crank
2. Pulling the hand wheel out to the right of the machine.
3. Pushing in a round divot inside the hand wheel (often seen on Singer® machines).

Some newer machines do not have a clutch release—once you push the bobbin winder toward a small metal or plastic guide located next to it (or even just place the bobbin on the winder), the machine knows you are winding a bobbin and will automatically release the needle for you. Again, check your manual.

With your spool in place on the spool pin, string the thread around the bobbin thread guide and through one of the holes in the side of the bobbin (have the thread come *from the inside* of the bobbin *to the outside* of the bobbin). Place the bobbin on the winder and hold the thread tail straight out with your right hand. Press the foot pedal to start winding, while still holding the thread tail in your fingers, keeping it away from the bobbin. After

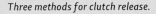
Three methods for clutch release.

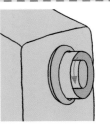 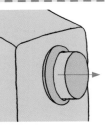 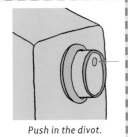

Crank the inner hand wheel.   *Pull the hand wheel out.*   *Push in the divot.*

pfaff

white
necchi
euro pro

bobbins

bobbins

foot

the bobbin spins around about 10 times (no need to count, a quick press on the foot pedal will get you there), let off the pedal and cut the thread tail at the outside of the bobbin. Make sure your tail does not get tangled in the bobbin. Now press the foot pedal and watch the magic of bobbin winding. Some machines will automatically stop when the bobbin is full but, just to be safe, you should stop winding when the bobbin is nearly full. You do not want thread to be wound beyond the edges of the bobbin.

Another method is to hand-wind the thread around the bobbin to get it started. String the thread around the bobbin thread guide and wrap the thread around the bobbin a few times by hand. Most bobbin winders wind clockwise, so make sure to place the bobbin on the winder with the thread running behind the bobbin.

A well-wound bobbin will feel firm when you poke at it with a pen or the end of your scissors; it should have the same consistency as the thread on your store-bought spool. If it's loose and bubbly, unwind it and start over. (Believe us—a poorly wound bobbin will cause you nothing but

headaches when you try to sew. And chances are that this amount of thread is less expensive than the amount of fabric it will mess up, so it's OK to unwind a little of it now.)

Good bobbin   *Bad bobbin*

LOADING THE BOBBIN

Front-loading machines use an external bobbin case, and the bobbin needs to be loaded into the case *before* the case can be loaded into the machine. Hold the case in your left hand with the "finger" pointing to the left and the open side facing you. Hold the bobbin in your right hand with the thread tail pointing in the opposite direction of the finger (figure 1).

Finger

Figure 1

This is important because loading the bobbin this way creates another point of tension in the system—and you know how we like tension. Place the bobbin in the case and pull the thread tail through the slit in the case (figure 2). Now run it underneath the plate until the thread comes out the hole in the side of the case (figures 3 and 4).

Inserting the bobbin in a front-loading machine

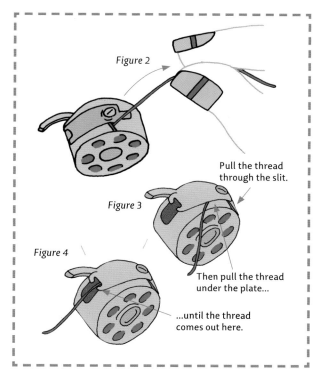

Figure 2

Pull the thread through the slit.

Figure 3

Figure 4

Then pull the thread under the plate...

...until the thread comes out here.

Insert the bobbin case into the machine while pulling out the lever (you are opening the "back door" of the bobbin, if you will) on the bobbin case. The finger should be pointing up. There is a certain spot where the bobbin case is secure in the machine; you should hear a click when the case hits this spot. Release the lever once the case is secure. If the case moves when you try to spin it with your finger, it is *not* secure. You *must* secure it before you begin sewing.

Top-loading machines do not have an external bobbin case. Hold the bobbin so the thread hangs down on the left side of the bobbin, making a P (figure 5), then drop it into place (figures 6 and 7). Lightly pull the thread back through the slit on the side—and you're done!

Inserting a bobbin in a top-loading machine

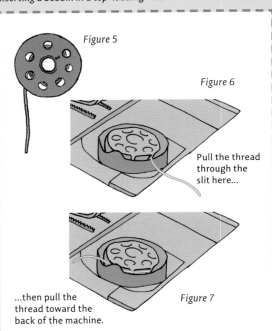

Figure 5

Figure 6

Pull the thread through the slit here...

...then pull the thread toward the back of the machine.

Figure 7

BRINGING UP THE BOBBIN THREAD

With the machine threaded from the spool all the way through the needle, hold the top thread tail loosely in your left hand and turn the hand wheel toward you with your right hand (figure 8)

until the needle goes down into the plate and back up. Notice that when you turn the hand wheel, the top thread is looping around the bobbin case (figure 9). This is the chaining action we talked about in "How a Sewing Machine Works" on page 21. Isn't it cool? (Hey, just call us sewing nerds.)

Stop turning the hand wheel when the thread up-take lever is at the top position and you see a small loop of thread just below the presser foot (figure 10). Take your scissors, a pen, or some other skinny object and pull the loop out. Both threads should sit below the presser foot and above the feed dog (like the meat part of a presser foot/feed dog sandwich)

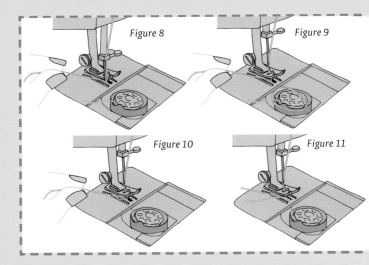

Figure 8

Figure 9

Figure 10

Figure 11

with the tails running behind and to the left of your machine (figure 11). You're ready to sew! Hooray!

STRAIGHT VS. ZIGZAG STITCHING

Sewing with straight stitches versus zigzagging isn't just about style or decoration—there is a functional purpose, too. You choose your stitch pattern based on the type of fabric you're using. (Check out "Fabric 101" on page 58 for more information on different types of fabric.) Generally, you use straight stitches on woven fabrics (fabrics that do not stretch) and zigzag with knit fabrics (fabrics that stretch). The reason for this distinction is that a zigzag stitch acts like a spring, allowing the stitch to stretch with the fabric. If you use a straight stitch on stretchy fabric, the thread can break (or the fabric can tear) because the stitch is unable to stretch with the fabric.

You tell the machine to make straight or zigzag stitches by selecting the desired stitch on the stitch pattern selector (see page 28). Some machines have separate stitch pattern selections for straight and for zigzag stitches. On other machines, the straight and the zigzag stitches are on the same pattern selection. If this is the case with your machine, a zigzag stitch with zero width is the same thing as a straight stitch.

It's a good idea to spend some time working with both the straight stitch and the zigzag stitch before you sew your first project. Find some scrap fabric (practice both zigzag and straight stitches on stretchy and nonstretchy fabrics) and play with the different stitch widths and lengths on your machine. This will familiarize you with the settings and increments of your particular machine.

While you're practicing, pay attention to the straightness of your stitches. Stitches need to be in a straight line whether they are straight or zigzag. As simple as that seems, be forewarned that sewing in a straight line is one of the hardest parts of sewing. Practice, and then practice some more. Hint: Use the right edge of the presser foot as a guide by running your fabric parallel to this edge.

CHANGING THE NEEDLE

At some point, you're going to break a needle. Not to worry! It's not that big of a deal—as long as you have spares. It's always smart to have plenty of extra needles on hand. It's even smarter to make sure they are the correct type of needle for your machine; consult your manual or just take the old needle to the fabric store to find a match.

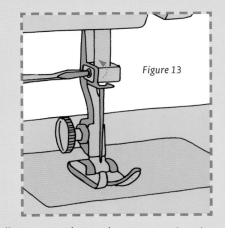

Figure 13

Figure 12

Depending on your machine, changing the needle sometimes requires a small screwdriver, but it can also be as simple as turning a little knob (figure 12) located above the needle, right where you'd think it would be. When you replace the

needle, you need to make sure to orient it correctly, so be sure to note the needle's position before you take it out. Usually, there is a flat area on the shank (the top portion) of the needle. This is the back of the needle, and it typically faces away from you (though you should check your machine's manual for specifics).

For machines that require a screwdriver to change the needle, there should be a tiny screw at the top of the needle. Turn the screw (righty tighty, lefty loosey) until the needle loosens (figure 13). Be sure to orient the new needle correctly when you insert it.

BACKTACKING

Backtacking is like buying insurance for your seams. Backtacking at the beginning and end of your stitch line ensures that your stitches won't pull out and your seam will be secure. To back-tack, use the reverse button, which is usually located at the front, lower right of your machine (see page 28). Stitch forward for about ¾ inch at the beginning of your fabric (no need to mea-sure), then press the reverse button while your foot pedal is still pushed down, and backtack, or sew backward over your seam to the beginning of the stitching. Then continue going forward (by releasing the reverse button) to complete your seam. Do the same backtacking at the end of the seam. In other words, the beginning and end of every seam will be sewn over three times.

TURNING CORNERS

Pillows, curtains, and place mats can all have sharp corners. To make your corners nice and square, finish your stitch with the needle in the fabric exactly at the corner. (If the needle isn't in the fabric at the end of your seam, use the hand wheel to reinsert it.) Lift up the presser foot and pivot the fabric around the needle to set up your next line of stitches. Lower the presser foot and continue sewing.

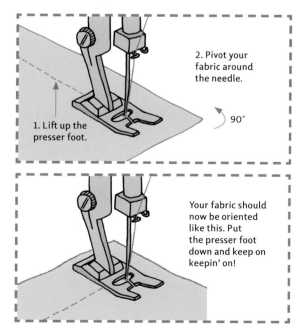

2. Pivot your fabric around the needle.

1. Lift up the presser foot.

90°

Your fabric should now be oriented like this. Put the presser foot down and keep on keepin' on!

WORKING THOSE CURVES

It can be difficult and intimidating to sew in a curve because doing so requires some control

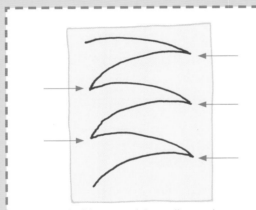

Pivot the fabric around the needle at each corner.

over the machine. But just relax and let yourself mess up. (Hey, it's sewing, not surgery!) You just need a little practice to make perfect curves. Start by taking a piece of scrap fabric and drawing some curves on it with a marker or tailor's chalk. Start with the pattern shown at top left. Try to follow the line of the pattern with your stitch. Remember in "Turning Corners," that you can change the direction of your seam by leaving the needle in the fabric, lifting the presser foot, and pivoting the fabric around the needle. You can also do this to realign the stitch if you find yourself going way off your marked line.

Once you have the curves and corners of this pattern mastered, move on to the more advanced spiral drawing at bottom left. This curve is harder to follow smoothly because the line is continuous, and your errors will show more clearly. But don't worry—you'll get the hang of it eventually. Sew slowly and keep practicing until you are satisfied that you can control the machine.

You now have the basic skillz to sew. Let's get your workspace ready!

GEARING UP
for Your First Sewing Project

Sewing—by hand or with a machine—requires the right equipment and the ability to use it. In this chapter, we'll spend some time talking about the tools and supplies you'll need to get your sewing hobby off the ground. We'll also teach you how to keep your stuff organized. (Those pinking shears aren't going to help you one little bit if you can't find them!)

Then, once you've practiced your sewing techniques (whether by hand or on a machine) and gathered your gear, it's time to roll up your soon-to-be-refashioned sleeves and start sewing. Let's make something, already!

THE GEAR

Whether you bought a new sewing machine, borrowed your mom's old favorite, or found one on the street outside your apartment (not uncommon in San Francisco), you're ready to start sewing, right? Heck, yeah! Before you can get the feed dog barking, though, you'll need to get some gear together.

Your local fabric store is a sure bet for stocking up. If you have never been to one before, check the phone book or an online directory. The smaller mom-and-pop shops may be a little more expensive, but we like to support local independent businesses whenever possible. They typically have a unique selection of fabric and supplies and are run by passionate people who invest their hearts and souls into bringing you amazing fabrics and sewing gear! Be sure to take advantage of this great resource.

Another option is to shop on the Internet. The prices are reasonable and the shopping is easy, as long as you don't mind the shipping costs and the wait time for your stuff to arrive. We also like fabric field trips to epicenters of fashion. If you can make it to Los Angeles or New York, both cities have amazing fabric stores (located in the garment districts) with bargain prices that make it worth the cost of the trip.

If you are a more adventurous shopper, are on a tight budget, or are not quite sure about this whole sewing thing, you can always go the secondhand route. Try looking for fabric and tools at thrift stores, garage sales, flea markets, and estate sales. There is no guarantee that you'll find what you need or that the gear will be high quality, but we have found some incredible bargains this way. Look for sales listing "sewing stuff" in their ads. You never know what treasures await!

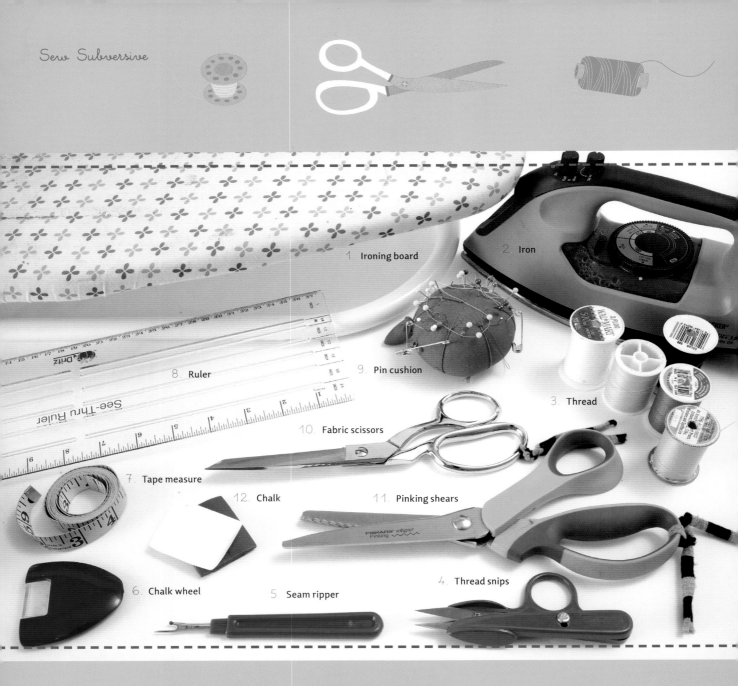

Sew Subversive

1 Ironing board

2 Iron

8. Ruler

9. Pin cushion

See-Thru Ruler

3. Thread

10 Fabric scissors

7. Tape measure

12. Chalk

11. Pinking shears

6. Chalk wheel

5 Seam ripper

4. Thread snips

FISKARS softgrip
Pinking

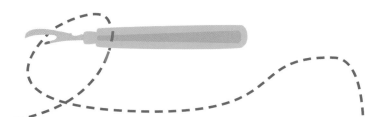

Our list of sewing essentials includes the following:

Fabric scissors (10)

Good scissors are a **must** for cutting fabric. You will find the scissors you need at a fabric store. They will cost more than the cheapies you can buy at the five-and-dime, but having sharp blades (that can be resharpened) will make your sewing life a lot easier. Be sure to use your good scissors *only* for cutting fabric. **Do not** use them on paper or anything else. It will dull the blades and make you sad. We learned from our moms that tying a small strip of fabric around one handle of your "fabric only" scissors helps remind you (and

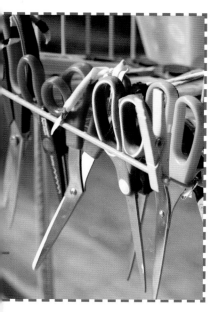

Remember: Safety first when storing your sewing blades!

your friends) which pairs are the good scissors and which pairs can be used to cut back the houseplants.

You can choose from different sizes, but you should select a pair that feels good in your hand. Large scissors are nice (and look pretty cool), but they may be difficult for you to work with if you're not used to long shears. The best bet for your first shears is a standard-size (8-inch) pair.

Pinking shears (11)

These scissors make that cool zigzag cut. Until now, you may have only used these to make fancy edges on paper cards for your friends, but now you'll finally know their true purpose! Pinking shears are used to cut woven fabrics with an edge that prevents unraveling. They are not totally nec-essary, but they can make working with wovens a lot easier. Plus, they're fun to use! Make sure to get a pair dedicated specifically for fabric and label them as you did your regular scissors, with a little strip of material.

Thread snips (4)

These little scissors are, sensibly, for snipping threads. Because of their size, they're easier to wield than regular scissors in many cases. They are not a requirement, but something that may make your sewing life a little easier. Keep these next to your machine for easy access when finishing a seam.

Ruler (8)

You could get away with using a yardstick, which you can usually pick up for free at your local hardware or fabric store, or you could spend a little money on a transparent grid ruler. The transparent ruler makes things easier because you can see the fabric underneath it, unlike the wooden yardstick.

Tape measure (7)

As you might imagine, it's long, looks like tape, and measures things. We're not talking about a retractable, construction-worker metal tape measure, but one made out of cloth or plastic. Picture a seamstress with one of these dangling around her neck. A tape measure is particularly

helpful when measuring yourself or your friend. A ruler isn't going to cut it when you're measuring your bust, unless you're shaped like a box. It's smart to own more than one tape measure, as it has a tendency to go missing (because you either set it down somewhere, or because your sewing partner thought it made the perfect belt for her new slip dress).

Chalk/chalk wheel (6, 12)

Your secret weapon! Tailor's chalk makes marks on your fabric that easily wash out or rub off. You'll use this to trace patterns or make marks where you want to pin or stitch. In particular, we like a tool called the chalk wheel. It's a little handheld plastic do-hickey that holds powdered

REFILLS FOR YOUR CHALK WHEEL

⭐ You can purchase refill cartridges from the fabric store. Just don't try to refill the cartridge using powdered chalk made for rock climbers or gymnasts—this chalk is not ground fine enough and will clog your chalk wheel. Take our word for it!

chalk and draws a line on the fabric with a wheel that releases the chalk. Refilling it can be a pain in the neck because of its small size (the white or blue powder can get everywhere). Try rolling up a piece of paper so you can use it as a funnel for the chalk—this helps a little, but it's still messy.

Straight and safety pins (9)

Longer straight pins with a ball on the end tend to be the easiest pins to work with, since you can get a good hold on them. Choose the kind with a glass ball—they are more expensive, but worth it since you can iron over them, which you can't do with the plastic-ended pins. Straight pins with flat metal ends are cheap but hard to work with, since there is not much to grab on to (you need finger-nails to get ahold of the ends to pull them out). They're more frustrating than anything. Straight pins come in different thicknesses. The thinner pins are better for pinning satin and other delicate fabrics, but they will usually bend if you use them on denim or canvas.

It's also smart to have a stash of safety pins among your sewing gear because they are stronger than straight pins. They also come in handy when you're pinning clothes while they're on your body and you don't want to (a) be stabbed when you remove the garment and (b) have your pins slip out after you've carefully positioned them. Another good use of safety pins is holding a seam together when you're low on time but *really* want to wear your new shirt tonight. (We only recommend this in the direst of circumstances.)

Pin cushion (9)

You need to have a place to put your pins when you pull them out as you're sewing (this will make more sense as you read further). You can go for the classic tomato pincushion, which is sometimes hard to use because its round bottom means it often runs around on the table as you try to stick pins in it with one hand. We also like magnets: They are easier to use because you can just drop the pin on top of the magnet. Fabric stores sell round plastic dishes with flat bottoms and shallow magnetic bowls that hold the pins as you set them down. We like to buy adhesive magnetic strips from the hardware store and attach them to our machines and/or sewing tables, which is cheaper and more convenient.

Iron (2)

A standard iron will meet most of your basic needs, but if you're serious about sewing, you may want to spend the extra cash and get a really good, über-hot iron that works on wool and heavier fabrics. If you're not sure how long your sewing phase will last, you can easily get by with a regular iron.

Ironing board (1)

Whether it's table-mounted or freestanding, you'll need an ironing board. You can get by ironing your pants on a towel on the kitchen table, but having

a sturdy, flat ironing board for prepping fabric makes things much easier (we explain this later in the chapter; read on).

Hand needles

Even if you're using the machine, you'll still need to sew by hand now and then. Sewing on buttons or accessing difficult spots will require your old-school skills, so keep some hand needles in your sewing stash.

Thread (3)

Grab some standard colors to get your collection started: white, cream, black, navy, brown, and fuchsia (hey, that's standard for some of us).

A NEAT THREAD TRICK

★ When you have your thread organized so you can see all your fabulous color options, create some special effects on your projects by using different colors for your spool and bobbin threads. Remember that the bobbin color is going to be on the bottom side of your material.

Thread racks make for convenient spool storage.

Don't worry about getting every color. When you start specific projects, you'll buy a spool to match the fabric, the leftovers will stick around, and you'll build up your thread collection that way. We prefer Gütermann® 100% polyester Sew-all thread—it's the most versatile for different fabric projects, and the thread is very high quality.

It's a good idea to organize your thread for storage. Interpret **organize** as you will, but keeping it all in one place with the ability to see all the colors in a single glance is a good place to start. You can purchase a thread rack, which looks very cool but takes up a lot of table space, or you can arrange spools inside a clear box (think resealable kitchenware) for a cheaper, stackable solution.

Seam ripper (5)

The seam ripper is every seamster's friend. This knifelike little tool is used to remove stitches. Even the best designers and seamsters mess up now and then and have to rip out seams. Some people like to use thread snips or scissors to do this, but seam rippers can be easier and are definitely more fun to use.

FABRIC 101

Like many new experiences, a shopping trip to a fabric store can be overwhelming at first, but once you find your way around and know what you're looking at, you'll feel like a kid in a candy store. Browsing for interesting fabrics can be an inspiring and fun way to get started on sewing projects. But you need to know what you're looking at, or what you're looking for, because not all fabrics behave the same, and some are better suited for certain projects than others.

Wovens & Knits

To keep the fabric talk relatively brief, we are limiting ourselves to two basic types of fabric: woven and knit. In general, woven fabrics do not stretch and knit fabrics do. Traditional denim (not the new cool stretch denim) and canvas are wovens. Jersey (like your T-shirt) and spandex are knits. Specialty fabrics like silk, corduroy, or velvet are not the best fabric for your first project. They are slippery and difficult to handle, and we want your first foray into sewing to be a pleasant one, not nerve-shattering. You can use those later, once you have honed your mad sewing skillz!

Wovens are easy to work with, especially when you're first learning to sew. They don't move, slip, or stretch in unexpected ways while you're working with them. They take pins very well, and they behave predictably.

Knits are great because they stretch and are more forgiving if you haven't fit the garment exactly to your proportions. At the same time, they are trickier to work with on the machine (because of that very same stretch).

When sewing a stretchy fabric on the machine, be sure to use a zigzag stitch and make sure the tension is correct. Practicing on some scraps of your fabric is important here, as you'll want to run several lines of stitches to get the tension just right (see page 26 for more on adjusting tension).

The most important thing to remember when sewing stretchy fabric on the machine is to resist the temptation to pull the fabric as it is moving across the feed dog. This may seem like a good shortcut—but it's not. The effect created by pulling the fabric toward you as it is being sewn is called lettuce edging (see "The Lettuce Edge" on the facing page). Although this is a feminine and cute way to finish an edge, it will cause much frustration if it is not the style you were going

Knit fabrics

A rainbow of woven options

for. Let those dogs do their job—*your* job is to hold the fabric steady in order to achieve a nice straight seam.

Like tool and supply shopping, you can go the new or used route when buying your fabric. If you have the money, buy new fabric. It's generally cleaner, and its fiber content is provided (i.e., 50% cotton/50% polyester, 100% cotton, and so on).

THE LETTUCE EDGE

★ By pulling stretchy fabric toward you while it is fed through the feed dog with a zigzag stitch, you can create a ruffle-like finish called a lettuce edge. This technique is to be used as a decorative element on your edges, not on internal seams. Ruffled

seams on your clothes don't lie flat and just add bulk. And we've yet to meet a seamster that wants her new, hot outfit to have additional bulk or lie funny.

Depending on your city, you may have a variety of fabric stores nearby, or you may be limited to just one. If you have a choice, check them all out (or ask a friend for a recommendation) before laying down your cash.

Shopping for fabric

Like clothing stores, fabric stores come in all levels: the cheap bargain-basement place with great remnants but little else, the really expensive store with a huge selection, the quirky place with crazy fabric that you've never seen before, and the old standard that is moderately priced and well stocked with the basics. We like them all. Each has an appropriate time and place in our sewing lives.

Another good reason to be familiar with your local stores is that you'll know about the year-end sales. Most have an annual clearance period when they purge their inventory for the new season's arrivals. This is a great time for fabric shopping!

No matter which store you frequent, make sure you know where to find the remnant bin. This gold mine offers precut pieces of fabric for deeply discounted prices (you can find anywhere from

One woman's remnant is another woman's treasure!

a fraction of a yard to 5 yards bundled together). The remnant bin is updated often, so check back every time you go to the store. Think of it as the clearance rack in your favorite retail store.

There is much to love about small pieces of fabric. You can use small patches as appliqués to add flair to your clothes. Think of repeated designs or logos on fabric that would look cool all alone on a plain shirt, skirt, or tote bag. Think about using different fabrics for the front and back of a pillowcase or even many different fabrics sewn together in pieces to create a patchwork design for a bag.

Although buying new fabric is reliable, buying used fabric is a great way to find some good deals. And as when thrifting for clothes, you're bound to find fabric that no one else has seen (at least for over a decade). We have found some estate sales selling yards and yards of fabric at a dollar a pop! Thrift stores often have a decent selection of fabric remnants—but remember to think outside the bolt. We've used bedsheets, curtains, blankets, pillowcases—even muumuus.

Estate sales can yield wonderful vintage fabric finds.

If it's big enough to cut a piece from, consider it fabric!

When you're shopping for fabric, touch it! You want to feel its texture and test the amount of stretch it has. Think, "How would this feel to work with? Is it stiff? Slippery? Might that cool pattern look funny when it's, say, stretched out over my rear end?" Shopping for fabric should be like shopping for clothes. Instead of "trying it on," you're "feeling it out" to see if it will meet your needs.

What are your needs? Good question. Sometimes we buy fabric that "speaks" to us, and we cannot possibly imagine another day of our lives without it, and other times the fabric is specifically slated for a particular project. In time, the fabric will tell you what it wants to be. It's like shopping for clothes—sometimes you need an outfit for a special date, and sometimes you need an outfit just because.

The party vs. the business side of fabric

Fabric has two sides; make sure you look at (and touch) both of them. You can think of one of the sides as the "party" side, or the fun side that will face the world when it is part of the finished product. Likewise, you can think of the other side as the "business" side, or the messy side where all your work happens, which will be on the inside of the finished product. Although fabric has an intended party and business side, sometimes the business is more interesting than the party, which may be inspiring

Here you can see the printed "party" side of the fabric versus the "business" side.

in and of itself! Think about how the business side will feel against your skin. Is it itchy? Will you need a lining? Consider using the party side on the front side on the front half of your shirt and the business side on the back.

Prewashing fabric

The rules are that you are supposed to wash your fabric, or "preshrink" it, before you sew. You really should. But because we sometimes forget to, or we just don't feel like going down to the Laundromat, in a pinch we will use the fabric anyway and make *sure* that we always wash the project in cold water, *forever*, so that it doesn't shrink. We leave the choice to you.

Ironing fabric

Generally, we think ironing is for other people. We buy clothes that don't need ironing and take the few items that do to the dry cleaner for pressing. Unfortunately, this philosophy doesn't transfer to sewing. Ironing before and during a sewing session makes life a lot easier.

After washing or pulling your fabric out of storage, it's a good idea to iron out all the wrinkles

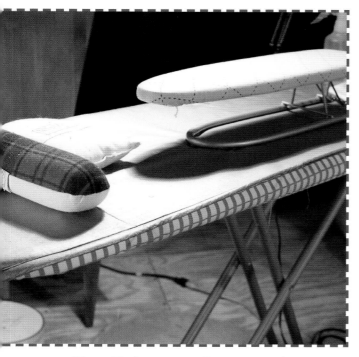

Hot off the press: Be sure to iron your fabric before and during sewing.

and folds. It's far easier than ironing clothing because unsewn fabric is a flat surface. Ironing fabric is like starting a painting with a clean canvas. Make sure you use the proper heat for your fabric: high heat with steam for most cotton wovens, low to medium dry heat for most everything else.

It is easier to iron on a legitimate ironing board than on top of a towel on the floor. The flat surface and the thin pad provide a consistent surface that won't create any patterns or unintentional wrinkles in your fabric. Use slow, long strokes and be sure not to leave the iron in any one place too long, or else the fabric may burn or melt. Use the steam function on cotton woven fabrics to get out the wrinkles.

Ironing is not only useful during preparation; you should also iron hems flat before stitching and iron seams open after stitching. Your hems will be straight, your seams will lie flat, and everything will have a nice, crisp finished look. Traditionally trained seamsters consider ironing a must, and it does make things look nicer, but realistically, you could get away without ironing. Your garment will still stay together, but it won't have that sharp, finished look. You decide how you want your piece to look. Is it a clean-cut skirt that would benefit from ironing, or is it a cut-up T-shirt that is meant to look like the clothing equivalent of "bed head"?

FABRIC 201: SHOPPING FOR REFASHIONABLE CLOTHING

We have already directed you to the secondhand outlets for fabric and notions, but while you're out thrifting, check out the clothes as well. The idea of taking an old piece of clothing and reconstructing it into something more "you" is what we refer to as refashioning.

When you're shopping for these hidden gems, it's important to keep your mind wide open. Look at the fabric, not necessarily the form. Usually the cut of clothing goes out of style for a reason. Don't get hung up on the tapered leg of a pair of pants; focus on the good areas and let your creativity redesign the parts that aren't screaming *you!*

Items that we usually buy include T-shirts, women's polyester blouses, pillowcases, sweaters, ties, dresses, and skirts. We like to shop at the discount thrift stores, not the expensive vintage stores. Remember, you are not looking for something that is ready-to-wear; you're looking for something you can give new life to. If you do find something that you like just the way it is, please buy it and wear it—you deserve the compliments for being in the right place at the right time!

Before you hit up the thrift stores, hit up your closet. We all are guilty of holding on to clothes we don't wear anymore. Find some of your favorites that you're not ready to let go of just yet, and work them into something new. Recycling your outdated fashion into a hipper version is a great way to fall back in love with a favorite shirt and hone your ability to see the refashioning potential in other clothes. Plus, there's no risk if you mess up—you weren't wearing it anyway!

NOTIONS: THE ACCESSORIES OF FABRIC

In addition to buying fabric or refashionable clothes, you'll need to pick up some other supplies during your shopping trip. Browse the massive selection of buttons, lace, ribbon, zippers, and patches (collectively referred to as "sewing notions") for anything that catches your eye. These don't have to be used for their intended purpose. Buttons make great embellishments even when they don't have a buttonhole to match.

Sometimes these small pieces can be all the inspiration you need for your next project, just as an amazing brooch can spark the idea for an entire outfit. No need to go crazy and overbuy in this department—chances are that this portion of your collection will build up on its own. These items are commonly found bundled together in thrift stores or garage sales, and there is usually one person in your family who has given up sewing and has a small collection ready to donate to your crafty cause.

Ribbon can be a great accent to a refashioned piece.

AFTER THE SHOPPING IS DONE

★ If you're like us, once your purchases are safe at home, the first thing you'll want to do is lay it all out and gawk your new collection, refashionable or otherwise! You should be proud of what you chose—after all, this is what you think is pretty/sexy/ hot/crazy/cool, so spend some time enjoying it. Just leaving your haul out for a day can trigger inspiration. We encourage you to care for it and store it—eventually—but there is certainly no harm in admiring your purchases for a while.

SETTING UP YOUR SEWING SPACE

Depending on your living situation, you may have an entire room you can devote to sewing, or you may be limited to one corner of your kitchen when your roommates are feeling particularly generous. Either way, you're going to need a table or worksurface on which to set your sewing machine and a stool or chair. Adjust the height of your worksurface and your chair so that the bottom of the machine is sitting somewhere between your elbow and shoulder when you are seated. The type of seat you choose can be very personal. Some people like stools; some prefer a chair with a backrest; others like sitting on exercise balls. Start with something you already have and make adjustments as your body dictates. Sit with good posture when you're sewing not only because it would make your grandmother proud, but also because you don't want a sore back from hunching over the machine.

Try to sit with your shoulders relaxed over your hips and your ears over your shoulders. Look down at your work with your eyes, not by bending your neck and back, though the sewing machine is like a face magnet and you're bound to find yourself right down by the needle at times. If you find yourself doing this, don't stress. Just stand up, stretch your arms up to the sky, take a few deep breaths, then return to your healthy sewing posture. Your body will tell you when it needs a break.

The cutting table at Stitch Lounge.

You will also need a flat place to lay out and cut fabric. Depending on your space, you may be lucky enough to have a specially designated cutting table. If so, position the height of your cutting table between your standing hip and elbow height. It shouldn't be so high that you have to climb onto it to reach the other side, but a table that is too low may cause you neck and back pain from bending over it.

If you're like most of us, you don't have enough space (or cash) to have a cutting table in your house. In this case, the dining-room table will do. Or, if that's not an option, the floor always works in a pinch.

KEEPING IT ALL TOGETHER

Like a fisherman, construction worker, artist, or chef, every seamster needs a toolbox. If you never leave the comfort of your home sewing room, you still need a place to organize and store your gear. Even if you are not the type who puts things away when you're done with them, we recommend finding a

We 💙 big bins for storage!

storage solution like a clear plastic bin or tool-box (the size will depend on how much gear you have). When you want to find those extra bobbins, you'll be happy you know where they live.

As for storing fabric, everyone has their preferred way. Some seamsters have piles of fabric sitting on the floor in their sewing room. Others categorize their fabric by color or type and store it carefully in clear stackable bins or on designated shelves. Being neat in this department means that when you're ready, you'll be able to find your fabric and know it's in good shape.

It's smart to store your notions in clear jars

Use your old cups and jars for handy (and cheap!) storage solutions.

A "dim sum" cart is a great storage solution for all your sewing notions.

Organize your bling in a clear plastic tray for easy access.

or boxes so you can easily see what you have. Spools of ribbons, cording, and lace can be hung on a string or rod for easy rolling access. You can buy fancy storage systems for your notions, but we've never done that. We prefer the "use what you've got" method.

HAVE GEAR, WILL TRAVEL

★ If you plan on sewing at friends' houses, schools, sewing circles, or lounges, then you must have some way of transporting your tools. Use this as an opportunity to show off your style. How you carry your gear can be an expression of your personality. Maybe it's a vintage lunchbox or suitcase, or perhaps a tackle box (remember Caboodles®?). You can purchase covered baskets from fabric stores specifically for this purpose, or you could even make your own.

★ As long as your tote is large enough to fit all your gear (so you don't have to lug around more than one bag) and it makes you happy, then it's perfect! Some seamsters like to carry around fabric or the current project they're working on, so

Pack your bags for your next sewing adventure.

they might use something larger, like a suitcase or backpack (with sections for organization, of course!). Remember, you don't have to bring everything with you wherever you go. You will always want your tools (scissors, hand needles, tape measure, seam ripper, and so on), but you don't have to bring all the materials you own. In other words, only bring the thread and notions you will need for your project—you can leave the rest of your collection safe at home.

MAKING SOMETHING

The tried-and-true way to learn about sewing is to practice. Then practice more. And then maybe practice some more for good measure. Start simple, and you'll begin to see what works and what doesn't. When things go less than perfectly, you'll figure out a better method the next time. (And maybe you'll get to use the seam ripper!) Remember that sewing is like any other activity; you have to practice to get better.

When you decide you're ready to tackle your first sewing project, start easy. Many people get excited about something they want to make and end up discouraged because they have taken on a project way above their skill level. It's best to build up your skills and confidence by beginning with something like curtains, a pillowcase, or a tote bag. Don't start your sewing career with a faux-fur coat or your cousin's wedding dress (unless you don't like her). Your first project may be inspired by a pattern you find or some fabric that you couldn't leave the store without. Many simple projects can be accomplished without a formal pattern.

It's important to have an organized plan before you start a sewing project. We're not talking organization like "having your bills in chronological order from the day you moved out of your parents' house." We're talking "cooking-from-a-recipe" organization. You need to make sure you have all the tools and supplies you'll need before you begin. You need to have a good idea of the pieces that make up the whole project and the order in which they will go together. Then visualize the steps you should follow in order to achieve the finished product.

MY FIRST SEWING PROJECT: PILLOW COVER

Making pillow covers isn't just a great way to start honing your sewing skills, it's a real money-saver! Never again will you think of tossing out the tired old throw pillows from your couch or bed and spending way too much on new ones. This basic sewing project will give new life to your old pillows by covering them with a simple envelope pillow cover.

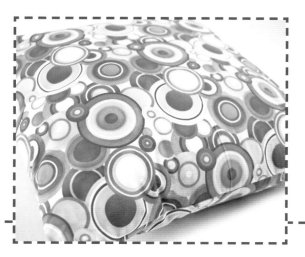

What you'll need
1 yard of fabric
  (woven, prewashed, dried, and ironed)
chalk
scissors
tape measure or ruler
thread to match your fabric
straight pins
iron and ironing board
hand needle or sewing machine

Techniques you'll use
running stitch, if hand sewing
straight stitch and backtack, if machine sewing

Time to complete
hand sewing: 1½ hours
machine sewing: 40 minutes

Step 1: Measure & cut

In order to know how much fabric you'll need, you need to first measure your pillow. The pillow in our example is 18 inches by 18 inches.

Take the width of your pillow and add 1 inch for seam allowance. This is the width of your rectangle (19 inches in our example).

Pillow width =
__ inches + 1 = __fabric rectangle width

Now take the length of your pillow, multiply it by 2, and add 7 inches: 6 for the overlap of the envelope cover (this will make more sense as you

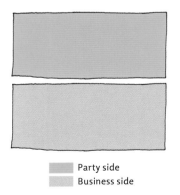

Party side
Business side

get further along) and 1 for hem allowance (43 inches in our example).

Pillow length =
(__ inches x 2) + 7 = __ fabric rectangle length

Use your chalk to mark the rectangle on your piece of fabric and cut it out. We cut out a 43-inch by 19-inch rectangle.

Step 2: Set up the machine

If your bobbin is empty, wind it full of the thread. Then load the bobbin and thread the machine. Make sure you have a medium-size needle, like an 11, and the rest of your supplies handy. Set your machine for a straight stitch with a medium length. Check your tension meter—you should be in the middle range. You're ready now!

If you don't have a sewing machine, you can hand-sew with a running stitch wherever we instruct you to use a machine.

Step 3: Fold, pin & iron the hems

Before you start sewing, it's smart to fold and pin any hems, then iron them down. This will make

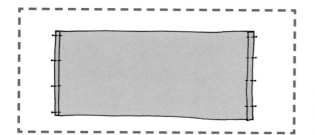

sewing easier, and the end project will look more professional. On each of the short ends of the fabric rectangle (the width), make a ½-inch fold and pin it down. Fold business side to business side, so that you can see the party side on the outside of your folds. Iron down the folded edges.

Step 4: Sew the hems

Pick one folded edge to start with and place the upper right corner under the presser foot. Keep

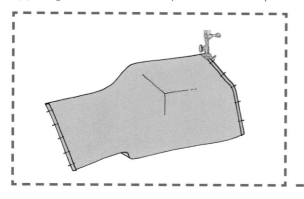

the excess fabric off to the left of the machine. Line up the folded edge with the right side of the presser foot.

Sew down this folded edge, remembering to backtack at the beginning and end of your line

POINTS ON PINNING

★ Pinning before you sew can be a huge time-saver during the construction phase of a project. *Note to self:* No sewing over pins! You should remove any pins you placed in your fabric before it runs under the machine needle. If you sew over a pin, it could shatter the needle (very dangerous!) and possibly even throw off your machine's timing. Many experienced seamsters sew over their pins, but we prefer to play it safe and remove them before they run under the needle. Also, always pin at a 90-degree angle to the seam, with the pin head coming out the right side—this makes it easier to remove the pin before it hits the needle. Pinning parallel to the seam would make pins difficult to remove, as the heads can get caught against the presser foot.

of stitches. Lift the presser foot, pull the fabric out to the left, and snip the threads close to the fabric. Do the same thing for the other folded edge. You should have a long rectangle of fabric with hemmed edges on the short sides.

Step 5: Envelope time!

Lay out your fabric with the party side up. Fold one end over so it overlaps the center of the rectangle length by about half of the width measurement; you're folding party side to party side, so you'll see the business side on the outside of the section you've folded. We folded over a 14-inch section in our example. Pin down this fold in a few places along the open sides of the fabric.

Now fold the other end over so it overlaps the first fold by 6 inches, leaving an 18-inch square. We folded a 10-inch section for this fold. Reposition the pins to hold down both folded edges. Make sure that the sides all line up, then iron down both folds to make nice even edges for sewing.

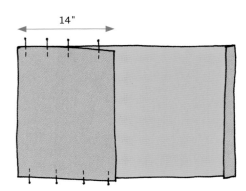

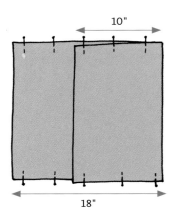

Step 6: Last bit of sewing

The machine settings and threading should stay the same. Place the top of one of the open edges (where you put your pins) under the presser foot, with the right edge of the fabric lined up with the right side of the foot. Sew a straight line down this open side, remembering to backtack at the beginning and end of the stitches. You are not sewing over your folds like you did in hemming. Instead, you are closing up the sides of the envelope. It's all coming together now, right?

Lift up your presser foot and snip your threads close to the fabric. Sew up the other side in the same manner.

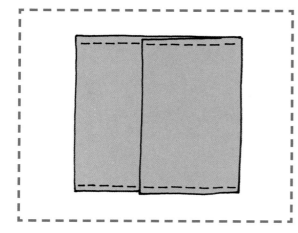

Step 7: All done!

Turn your new, fantastic pillow cover right-side out. Poke inside the corners with the eraser end of a pencil or the end of a pen to make them sharp. *Voilà!* Slip your old throw pillow into this fabulous new cover and make sure to show it off as often as possible! Way to go, you finished your first sewing project!

MESSING UP

Face it—you're going to mess up at some point. It's just the way it is when you're learning a new skill. Just remember that everyone makes mistakes and that mistakes are not a waste if you learn something from them (now we really sound like our mothers!). When a project doesn't go exactly as planned, don't toss it in the trash. Think about why it might have gone wrong and what you could have done differently for a better result.

Most of the time you can fix your mistakes, but if you can't, try to think creatively. Our mantra is, "Everything can be turned into a tube top."

So go out there! Sew! Be creative! Mess up! Sew some more! And most of all—have fun!

MAKING IT YOUR OWN:
Embellishing + Customizing Clothes

It's time to tackle our favorite stuff—clothes and how to make them your own. In this chapter, we're going to be adding to and changing garments that need a little pizzazz, making them just right for you. We will also cover simple refitting techniques for skirts that are too big and shirts that are too small. Think of these changes as the sprinkles on your ice cream, the olives in your martini. You are bound only by your imagination.

A sewing machine is not required for any of these projects, but using one will save you time on the projects that involve sewing. And you'll see that, even without a lot of sewing skill, it's easy to start subverting fashion your way.

MAKE YOUR PRINTER WORK FOR YOU

Find a cotton T-shirt that fits you well, but needs a little pop. Find a noncopyrighted image on your computer that you want to use to adorn your clothing. (Try to avoid things like company logos or famous art and drawings. Your safest bet is to stick with your own art creations. Be proud and show the world what you made! You can also use text if you don't have a picture you love.) You are essentially going to print your chosen image onto transfer paper and iron it on the T-shirt—like a cosmetic patch that adds a little funk.

Iron-ons are great for a variety of uses— to cover up a stain, personalize a shirt, make an old (but still clean) shirt into a new gift. You can even iron them on cotton underwear to make hot panties! These make great gifts—when the panties are new, of course. For example, a certain sister got a set of customized panties for her wedding shower—one with a picture of her betrothed, another with his name inside a heart tattoo, one with their wedding date and "Just Married," and (our personal favorite) one with a picture of her cat, Maggie, on the hip. Get creative!

Before we get started, crop and size your picture just the way you want it to appear and make a test print on regular paper to check it. Does it look hot? Then we are ready to play!

What you'll need

T-shirt

noncopyrighted image

ink-jet printer (no fancy laser printers; they melt the paper)

T-shirt transfer paper (sold at office supply and craft stores)

iron and ironing board or large towel

pillowcase (or other fabric)

83

AN IMPORTANT NOTE ON TRANSFER PAPER

★ There are a variety of types of transfer paper out there. Some of them are for white T-shirts only, and they are essentially clear paper that your image will be printed on. If you try to iron these onto a dark T-shirt, the image will blend into the background color of the shirt. Transfers also generally require that your image be flipped horizontally before printing—like a mirror image. This can either be done in the photo-editing software or as an option on your printer.

★ If you want to use a colored shirt, make sure you get transfer paper made specifically for use with dark shirts. The paper will likely be white (to create a break from the dark shirt so you can see the color). We've seen a variety of these papers, and sometimes they don't require the image to be flipped, as you peel off a backing and tack on the image like a sticker before you iron it. You can use this kind of transfer paper on white shirts as well. Just make sure you read *all* the instructions that accompany the paper, then read them again. They're not always clear the first time.

Techniques you'll use
ironing

Time to complete
45 minutes

Step 1:
Read all the instructions on the transfer paper packet and make sure your test print looks good to you. Then check that you can answer all these questions with a resounding "Heck, yeah!" before moving on.

★ Do you have the right transfer paper for the color shirt you'll be putting the image on (see "An Important Note On Transfer Paper")?
★ If the transfer paper you're using requires that you flip the image, have you done that?
★ Have you read all the instructions included with the transfer paper?
★ Is your image properly sized?

Step 2:
Print your image on the transfer paper according to the manufacturer's instructions and the printer

you are using. Then go grab a latte while you let your print dry.

Step 3: Ready your image

Cut out the image and trim the extra edges to your liking. (Keep in mind that if you don't trim the edges, they will generally show, either as a big white shape or as a clear texture on your shirt. Just trust us and trim.) Put on the shirt you're using, then hold the image up to where you want it to make sure you like how it looks. Take the shirt off, lay it down flat on your ironing board or a towel draped on a table, and place the design where you want it.

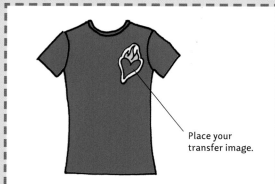

Place your transfer image.

Step 4: Get your iron on

Generally, you would be told to do a test iron on a shirt you don't like, but now that you are rolling with the subversive posse, we're going to assume you'll be fine without a tester. (But if you do want to do a test, now is the time to grab a spare shirt that you are comfortable playing around with.)

Now follow the manufacturer's instructions and get your iron on! All the papers are different, so it's very important that you follow the specific guidelines provided, but generally this will involve peeling off the back (for colored paper), covering it up with fabric or a protective sheet provided, and ironing. But you must check the instructions specific to your transfer.

Step 5: Be cool

And by "be cool" we mean "let it cool." This is the step lots of people try to skip, and it gives them smudgy results. Don't be one of those people. Once the transfer is cool to the touch, peel off the top paper or fabric, and *voilà!* You have a shirt that screams your name! (Now read the packet for washing instructions.)

A SKIRT THAT IS SEW YOU

Find a skirt that fits you well, but is plain or not quite your style. Maybe it was your style when you bought it, but it just hasn't kept up. You'll also need a patch or a cutout from some other fabric (think of the funny logo from an old T-shirt, a cool design on a fabric remnant you found on sale, or a funky pattern from an old pillowcase). Find something that inspires you and makes you smile.

What you'll need
skirt
patch(es) or fabric cutout(s)
straight (or safety) pins
thread (either matching your fabric, or the edge of your patch, or contrasting both)
hand needle or sewing machine
scissors

Techniques you'll use
blanket stitch, if hand sewing
straight stitch, backtacking, and turning corners, if machine sewing

Time to complete
hand sewing: 30 minutes
machine sewing: 15 minutes

Step 1: Cut your patch out

If you are using a ready-made patch (like a name tag from a vintage bowling shirt or an old Girl Scout badge), you can skip this step. If you want to work with a T-shirt logo or a portion of some fabric, carefully cut out the part that you will attach to your skirt.

Step 2: Pin it on

Take your skirt and decide where you will sew on the patch. Keep in mind that this patch will draw attention and, if there is writing on it, people might want to get close enough to read it. For that reason, you might not want to place it right over your rear end (or maybe you do! We're not here to stop you!). Once you have a spot selected, pin the patch to the skirt in a

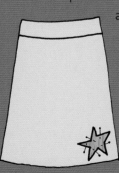

couple of places so it won't slip or rotate while you're sewing. We pinned our patch to the bottom right side of the skirt.

Step 3: Sew it on

Thread your needle with about an arm's length of thread. You'll be using the blanket stitch to sew on the patch. Since you'll be sewing all the way around the patch, you can start anywhere. If you run out of thread, just make a series of slip knots (see page 11) and start over with another arm's length of thread.

If you have a simple-shaped patch or cutout, you can use a straight stitch on your sewing machine, making sure to backtack at the beginning and end and pivoting your corners. This only works on the machine for items like skirts and T-shirts—pant legs are generally too narrow and bulky to slide onto your sewing machine arm.

Step 4: Finish it

Take your pins out and admire your work. Feel free to repeat that last part as often as you want.

TOPSTITCHING: DRAWING WITH THREAD

Topstitching is a simple method of embellishing your clothing by sewing on top of the fabric—meaning you're not sewing anything together. You can turn a plain shirt, skirt, pants, or jacket into a piece customized to your individual style. Shirts and skirts are easier to topstitch because you can easily get them in the machine. Pants are trickier because you need to be sure you only topstitch a single layer of fabric. It's pretty tough to put on pants when the legs have been topstitched together. If you can dream it, you can topstitch it: your initials, a plaid or argyle pattern, circles, stars, arrows—you get the idea. Try using thread colors that contrast with your garment so the decoration really stands out. Or you can use a thread that matches your garment so you'll see the texture but the color will blend in.

This is the time to have fun with the different stitch patterns on your sewing machine. Try out the straights and zigzags in different stitch lengths and widths. If you've got them, play with some of the other funky stitch patterns. But make sure you experiment on scraps. Start with straight lines, then try turning some corners to make other shapes. Once you get the hang of it, step it up a notch and try your hand at curved lines or circles. You can also take a pencil or chalk and draw something on the fabric, then trace the lines with your topstitching. This is a great way to get the feel for different forms.

Don't limit yourself to a design that is concentrated in one spot. Think about drawing lines around the bottom of a shirt, then adding a little decoration in the top corner. Or how about some vertical lines down the side of a skirt? The only thing to remember here is that if you're topstitching on stretchy fabrics ("knits" for those keeping score at home), the stitching will break if you stretch it too far. For instance, you would not want to topstitch around the circumference of a fitted cotton/lycra shirt. As soon as you pull it over your head and shoulders, your thread will break, and you'll be bummed.

In our example, we take a plain ol' button-down shirt and funk it up a bit with some contrasting topstitched patterns.

What you'll need

plain button-down shirt (or whatever you want to topstitch on)
chalk
thread (we are using two colors that stand out against the color of the shirt)
sewing machine

Techniques you'll use

any stitch you want
backtacking
turning corners
sewing curves

Time to complete

(this depends on your topstitch design; ours is pretty simple)
20 minutes

Step 1: Pick a spot

Decide which part of your plain ol' shirt would make a nice blank canvas for your design. Decide how big it should be. You can either make mental notes of this or sketch it out on a scrap piece of paper. We decided to topstitch the entire right front panel of the shirt.

Step 2: Plan a pattern

Take a blank sheet of paper and roughly sketch the front of the shirt, then draw in what you want the topstitched pattern to look like. We used two different colors since we'll be using two colors of thread. This will give you a good idea of how your design will look. We decided to go with intersecting straight lines in one color and circles topstitched over that in the second color.

Step 3: Topstitch like a bandit

If your design is complicated, you may want to sketch it on the shirt with the chalk to have something to trace. We did this for the circles in our pattern.

With a spool of thread and matching bobbin thread loaded in your machine, place the shirt under the presser foot and start with the vertical lines. Inspect your stitches to make sure your tension is set correctly. These stitches are the whole project, so if they are too tight or too loose, stop to adjust the tension before you keep going. (*Hint*: Stitch each line twice for maximum impact.)

Next, go over the top of the vertical lines with some intersecting horizontal lines, still using the same thread color. Make some lines with straight stitches (medium stitch length) or zigzag stitches (change the stitch width and length for variety between lines). Make sure to backtack at the beginning and end of the lines. Even though these stitches are not holding your garment together, you'll be sad if the threads come out and your design starts unraveling.

Now reload the bobbin and thread the machine with the second color. Make some circles over the lines. It is easier to use a straight stitch for the circles. Don't forget to backtack!

When you're done with your masterpiece, trim all the threads nice and neat, and you're set.

BYE-BYE BORING BRITCHES

Your canvas for this project is a pair of pants that fits you well, but needs a little flair. Your detailing will stand out if you choose pants made from a plain fabric, but those constructed from a wildly decorated fabric can also look great with some subtle embellishments. In addition to your britches, you're going to need some ribbon or lace, or, if you really want to get crafty, try cutting strips of fabric to use instead of ribbon (just be sure to cut straight lines!). The ribbon/lace/strips of fabric can either match or contrast with your pants; this is the part where you turn your pants into *your* pants.

What you'll need
pants
tape measure
straight (or safety) pins
ribbon, lace, or fabric strips (about 4 yards)
thread (either matching or contrasting your ribbon)
hand needle
scissors

Techniques you'll use
running stitch

Time to complete
1 hour

Step 1: Measure it
Using your tape measure, measure the waistband of your pants. When you sew on the ribbon, you don't want to cover any buttons, so if your pants have a button or other type of closure,

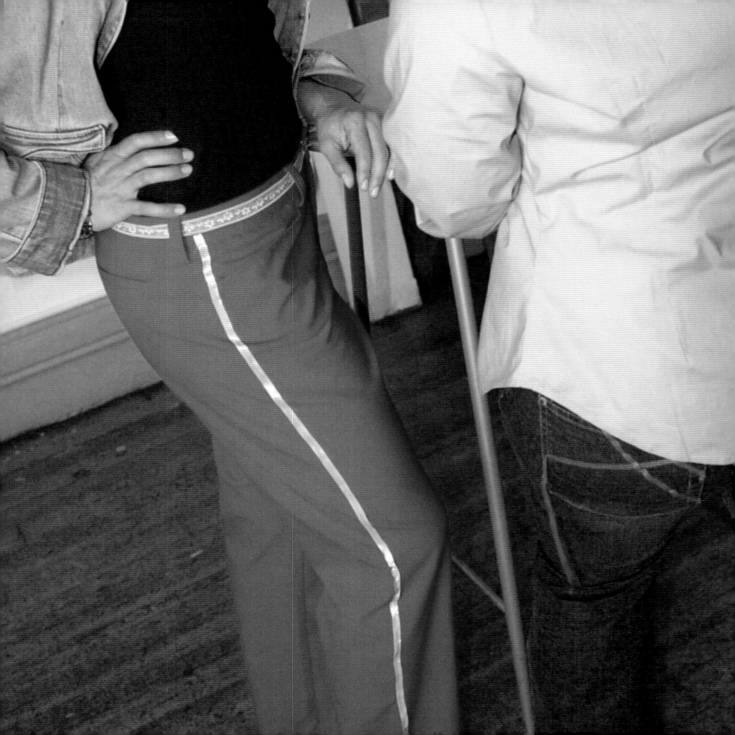

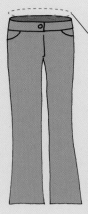

Measure length of waistband.

measure from one side of the closure, around the back of the pants, to the other side of the closure, excluding the button area. Add 1 inch to this measurement for hemming. We will call this piece the "waistband" in our directions.

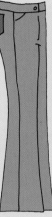

Measure from the top of the waistband...

...to the bottom of the leg.

Now measure from the top of the waistband on one leg all the way down to the very bottom in a straight line. Add 1 inch to this for hemming. We'll call this measurement the "leg."

Waistband = __ inches + 1 = __ inches
Leg = __ inches + 1 = __ inches

Step 2: Cut the ribbon

You're going to cut three pieces of ribbon: one waistband and two legs. If you think you may have measured incorrectly, measure again just to be sure. We don't mean to sound like our moms, but always "measure twice, cut once." You can also always add another inch, just to be safe.

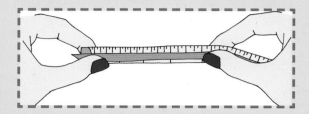

Hold your tape measure alongside the ribbon to measure out the correct lengths for cutting.

Step 3: Pin it

Grab a couple of pins and one of the leg ribbons. Take one end of the ribbon and fold the end over so you have ½ inch folded on the back side of the ribbon. (When the ribbon is sewn on the pants, the folded end won't fray and look shabby.) Pin

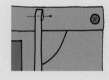

the folded edge to one side of the waistband (usually right next to or on top of the side seam) at the top of the band.

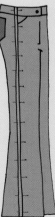

Lay the ribbon flat down the side of the pant leg and pin it a couple more times along the leg of the pant. Finally, fold the free end of the ribbon over just like you did at the top and pin this end to the very bottom of the pant leg.

95

Step 4: Sew it

Thread your needle with about an arm's length of thread. You'll be using the running stitch to sew on the ribbon. Start at the top and sew across the top edge of the ribbon, then begin sewing down one side of the ribbon. You will sew all the way down, around the folded edge at the bottom, and back up the other side of the ribbon until you get back to where you started.

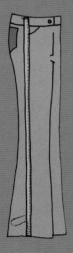

This is a lot of stitching, and you will most likely need to rethread your needle at least once during this process. When you're getting close to the end of your thread, secure the seam by tying a series of knots (see page 11) and start over with another arm's length of thread. Use these knots to finish off your stitches when you're all done as well.

Step 5: Finish it

Take your pins out and pat yourself on the back for rocking the running stitch!

Step 6: Repeat it

Repeat steps 3, 4, and 5 on the other leg. Then repeat steps 3, 4, and 5 for the waistband. When you sew on the waistband, you'll be sewing

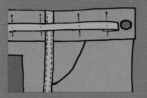

Pin the waistband.

over the top of the leg ribbons, for a finished look. You'll pin and sew your folded ribbon ends to either side of the button or snap.

Step 7: Model it

Put those babies on and find yourself a full-length mirror. Make sure to admire yourself from *all* angles, because everyone else will!

CUT IT OUT! SHIRT

When a shirt is just too much—and you want to show off a little skin—you need to just cut it out! No, we mean it! Get rid of the fabric by cutting a shape or pattern into the shirt and show off your beautiful, glowing skin. It's optional, but we recommend that you topstitch the pattern onto the shirt before cutting out the shape inside the topstitching; doing this will keep the fabric from rolling after you've cut it.

What you'll need
stretchy T-shirt (short- or long-sleeved)
scissors
thread (if you want to topstitch)
sewing machine (if you want to topstitch)
sunscreen for your newly exposed skin
    (SPF 15, please!)

Techniques you'll use
cutting
topstitching (optional)

Time to complete
10 to 30 minutes

We turned this tee into a tank and didn't bother topstitching.

Step 1: Decide the two w's: where and what

Think about what you'd like to do with your shirt. Cut a keyhole to show off your décolletage? What about a subtle leaf pattern to reveal a hint of shoulder? Don't pick a shape that's too complicated, because you're going to have to cut around it. We're going to show you one example with topstitching and one with a clever keyhole.

Step 2: Sew it up

If you are topstitching, get going! (If not, you can skip this step.) Topstitch your design onto the shirt. Pick large shapes that will provide sizable sections for you to cut out. We like ovals and circles and squares. Also keep in mind that you'll be cutting material out, so you cannot sew a shape inside another shape you intend to be cut out. For example, a happy face would not be a good choice because as soon as you cut out the face, the eyes go with it!

Cut out the material inside your stitching, about $\frac{1}{8}$ inch away from the thread, making sure you don't cut the thread itself. If you decided not to topstitch, this is your time to just get cuttin'! Find a clever shirt or one with a design already on it that has a spot screaming for a cutout. Since material tends to roll once it's been cut, use that to your advantage. You could take a stretchy long-sleeved shirt and cut a series of 3-inch horizontal slashes down the arm, about $\frac{1}{2}$ inch apart. The material should roll up a little once it's been cut, showing a little skin and adding a little pizzazz.

— Topstitch
-- Cut along dotted line

Step 4: Show it off!

Slather on the sunscreen, pull on your shirt, and show the world what you've just created!

Freeform stitching can yield eye-catching results...

ALL EARS—OR HORNS—HOODIE

Hooded sweatshirts (aka hoodies) are awesome. They are super-flexible—zip to keep yourself warm, unzip to cool off—and the delightful hood, when pulled up, makes you look even more charming. Well, we took something cute and made it even cuter. Pink hoodie, meet your future: kitty hoodie.

Yes, we're grown-ups, but we still love to wear things with a little surprise. This looks like a normal hoodie, but zazz . . . it's not! It's got adorable little kitten ears. And you don't have to stop there. You can make dinosaur spikes, devil horns, bunny ears—the possibilities are endless! Luckily, we like to do things the easy way, so we don't plan on having you make your own hoodie. There are lots of good, plain hoodies out there that are screaming for adornment. Caution: This is likely to become your favorite item of clothing!

What you'll need

hooded sweatshirt, preferably with a zipper, but nonzippered hoodies will do

scraps of felt for ears (or spikes) that match—or contrast with—your hoodie (these can be taken from the remnant bin)

chalk

seam ripper (for dinosaur hoodie)

straight pins (for dinosaur hoodie)

scissors

thread (to match your hoodie)

hand needle or sewing machine

iron and ironing board

Techniques you'll use

running stitch, if hand sewing

straight stitch, backtacking, and turning corners, if machine sewing

Time to complete

hand sewing: 30 to 60 minutes

machine sewing: 20 to 40 minutes

The Melicat and the Hopeasaurus aren't the only games in town. Get mischievous with the kitty pattern—make devil horns instead of ears!

Step 1: Pick an animal (prehistoric or not!)

Decide what you'd like to transform your hoodie into. We're going to walk you through two versions: Melicat (two ears on the sides of the hood) and Hopeasaurus (several spikes down the middle of the hood). You can piggyback the concept of either of these to customize your hoodie to your little heart's desire. We'll be using a pink hoodie with pink and white felt for the Melicat, and a green hoodie with green felt for the Hopeasaurus.

Step 2: Cut your ears and spikes

Melicat: Decide how large you'd like your ears to be. Ours are about 2½ inches tall and shaped like a triangle. Don't cut yet! You will need to add a seam allowance and a ¾-inch anchor to your ear; the anchor gives you something to sew to the hoodie. Since the ears are small, we're going to use a ¼-inch seam allowance for the edge of the ear. (Any larger and the extra material would prevent you from having pointy ears—who wants that?) Cut out four ears the same shape

Ear ➤

◄ Anchor

and size from the pink felt.

Now cut out two smaller triangles from the

white felt, without the anchor, to represent the fuzzy inside of the ear. (If you are feeling crazy, you can use faux fur instead of felt, but you must always wash it on cold and line dry or your fur will get a little matted.) Pin the white triangles to the top of two of the pink felt pieces, so that the bottom of the white triangle ends above the anchor. Hand- or machine-sew them down, using white thread. After the ears are attached, the bottom of your white triangle should line up with the bottom of your pink triangle, as the anchors will be hidden under your hood.

Hopeasaurus: Decide how many spikes you'd like to have going down the back of your head. We recommend between five and ten. The general rule is, the bigger the spikes, the fewer you should have. You will need two triangles with anchors for each of your spikes, so cut out twice as many triangles as the number of spikes you want. Feel free to vary the size of each triangle if that is how you roll.

Step 3: Sew your ears and spikes

Sew your pairs of triangles together ¼ inch in from the edge, but only sew on the angled edges—don't sew the anchor edges together, as you will need to separate them and attach them to the hood. In general, felt is the same on both sides, so there is not a party side or business side—it's all party! For the Melicat, however, the white triangle side is your party side, so make sure it faces the other piece of felt (you'll be turning the ear right-side out).

Sew the triangles together party side to party side.

Step 4: Flip it

Turn your triangles right-side out, so you no longer see the seam. Stick something into the triangle (like a pencil) to push the point out to

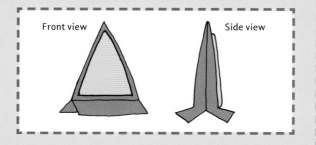

Front view   Side view

make those ears as kittylike as possible. Iron your ears down (the felt ones, please!) to flatten the seams.

Step 5: Check it out

Figure out where you'd like your ears and spikes to go. Mark the spot with chalk.

Melicat: Cut two small slits where you want your ears to go on the hoodie.

Slip the ears through the slits from the inside of the hood so only the triangle is sticking out, white side facing forward, with the anchors spread out inside the hood. Sew around the bottom of the ear, through both the hood and the anchor, to secure your ears in place, making sure to backtack.

Hopeasaurus: After marking your spike

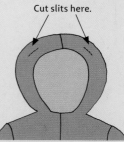

Cut slits here.

Insert the ear into the slit from inside the hoodie.

Sew down the anchors inside the hoodie.

103

Flip the hoodie inside out and rip open the center seam.

■ Party side
□ Business side

After splitting your hood down the middle, it should look like this when laid flat.

Party-side-to-party-side spike sandwich

placements on the side of the seam (make sure it's on the side so you can still see them after cutting), split open your hood at the middle seam. You can use a seam ripper for this or you can cut it down the middle. Keep in mind your hood will be a little smaller when you are finished, due to seam allowances.

Place your spikes at your markings on one of the party sides of the hood, with the spikes facing inside. Lay the other party side of the now-split hoodie on top of the spikes for a party-side-to-party-side spike sandwich, if you will, and pin it together.

Sew ½ inch in from the edge, starting at the neck of the hoodie, all the way up to the top. Make sure to backtack.

Step 6: Show your stuff!

Melicats and Hopeasaurus, flip your hood the right way out, put on your hoodie, and let out your biggest meow and Hopeasaurus roar! And now see if anyone can possibly resist your cuteness. They won't be able to. We promise.

FROM BIG + BAGGY TO FIT + FLATTERING

Here we'll take you through the steps of turning a skirt that's a little too big into something that fits a little better. The technique we're describing is sometimes called a "pin tuck." A pin tuck is basically a narrow fold of fabric that sticks straight up when sewn together, giving a decorative look to a garment but also serving to take in a little material. (We are all about techniques that are cute and practical.) This can be used on shirts, too.

We recommend you use a sewing machine for pin tucks because you'll need the stitches to be straight and even, since they will be visible. Sewing machines often have a pin-tuck foot—a flat foot with grooves cut in the bottom—that you can use, but it's not necessary.

What you'll need

lightweight, mostly cotton skirt (not denim), with a side or back zip (no elastic or drawstring—they would get sewn into the fold)

thread (this will be visible, so either use the same color as the skirt or something that will look cool contrasting)

iron and ironing board

sewing machine

Techniques you'll use

straight stitch

backtacking

Time to complete

1 hour

Step 1: Size it up

Measure how big your skirt is and how much smaller you'd like it to be. Since each pin tuck is like a little two-sided ridge, it takes up twice the amount of fabric as its height. For example, a ¼-inch pin tuck will take in about ½ inch of fabric. Generally, we keep our pin tucks around ¼ inch. (But that's just us, if you want a bigger or smaller one, do it!) Anyway, if you want your skirt to be an inch smaller, it will have two pin tucks, each taking up a ½ inch of fabric and standing ¼ inch tall (1 inch ÷ ½ inch of fabric = 2 pin tucks, each ¼ inch tall). You can pinch the fabric a little to see how a pin tuck will look.

Step 2: Get decisive

Now that you know how many pin tucks you need, you have to decide where to put them. Keep in mind that pin tucks are meant to take in small amounts of fabric, but they do add up if you put lots of them in. So use your pin tucks judiciously.

With the skirt right-side out, fold the fabric where you want the ridge of the pin tuck to be. Iron down that ridge. That will be where your first pin tuck will live.

Iron down the pin-tuck ridge.

Step 3: Tuck

Front of skirt

Side seam of skirt

Starting at the waist, stitch a line ¼ inch in from the ridge, using the outer edge of your presser foot as a guide. Sew all the way down the edge of your fabric, remembering to backtack.

After you finish sewing your tuck and cutting off loose strings, press the skirt flat again and try it on with your new pin tuck. If it's still too big, repeat until you have the proper number of tuck lines and a deliciously fitting skirt!

Pintucks aren't just for skirts—try it on a shirt!

HONEY, I SHRUNK THE SHIRT!

You'd think we'd all know better than to put a fitted cotton shirt in the dryer on high heat. Inevitably, despite being the fabulous ladies we are, we still manage to shrink—or our partners manage to shrink—our clothes on occasion. Here we'll show you how to add some fabric to a shirt that is too small, making it wearable again. This can also apply to shirts that you may have grown out of or shirts from a local thrift shop that, while a bit too snug, had such unbelievable cuteness that you simply could not ignore them.

Find yourself a shirt that's just a little too tight for comfort (or to wear in public). It can be short or long sleeved, or it can be a tank top (a tank is actually easier to work with). We don't recommend trying this with a button-down dress shirt, at least not on your first attempt. Start with something simple made from cotton or polyester knit fabric (which has some stretch to it, so it is a bit more forgiving).

What you'll need

shirt
fabric for panels (less than ¼ yard—a
    remnant or scraps should work fine)
seam ripper
tape measure
ruler
chalk
scissors
straight pins
thread (to match either your shirt or your
    add-on fabric)
hand needle or sewing machine

Techniques you'll use

running stitch and hemming, if hand sewing
straight stitch and backtacking, if machine
    sewing

Time to complete

hand sewing: 3 hours
machine sewing: 2 hours

You're also going to need some fabric to add to the sides and under the arms of the shirt. Choose fabric that is of a similar weight and feel as the shirt. What it looks like is up to you. We've chosen to use a cute fabric for the additional panels to jazz up the shirt we started with.

Step 1: Make a plan

Figure out how much fabric to add to your shirt to make it comfortable again. Use your tape measure to measure around your torso at the widest spot (this is generally your bust, but it could be a pregnant belly, too). Hold your tape loosely around your body because you are marking where you would like your shirt to fall when this is all done (not how the shrunken shirt fits currently). Make a note of this measurement. Next, lay your shirt flat and measure the width of the torso from side seam to side seam. Multiply that

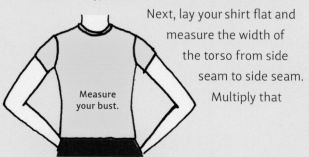

Measure your bust.

Measure the torso width of your shirt from side seam to side seam.

number by 2 and subtract this measurement from your bust measurement. This is the total number of inches that you'll need to add to the width your shirt.

My bust = __ inches

My shirt = __ inches x 2 = __inches

My bust – my shirt =__ inches that need to be added

Step 2: Prep the panels

Since you will be adding the panels to the under-arms and down the sides of the shirt, you need to figure out how long to cut the pieces. Measure from the end of the sleeve (or the top of the tank top, in the armpit) along the seam of the shirt, to the bottom of the shirt. Add 1 inch to this measurement for hemming and write it down.

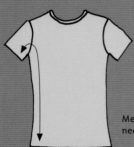

Measure the length you need for your side panels.

Length from sleeve end to bottom = __ inches + 1 = __ inches (length of panel)

To figure how wide to make the panels, refer back to the math you did in step 1. Divide the number of inches you need to add to your shirt by 2 (since there will be a panel added on each side) and add 1 inch for seam allowance. This will be the width of each of the panels.

__ inches to add to my shirt ÷ 2 = __ inches + 1 = __ inches (width of panel)

BEWARE: These measurements will add an equal number of inches to your bust, arms, and waist, so the arms and waist will get bigger, too. Don't use this strategy on shirts that only don't fit well in the bust—use it on shirts that need to be a little bigger all over.

Step 3: Cut the panels

Lay out the fabric you've chosen for the panels. Using your ruler and the measurements from step 2, draw chalk lines on the fabric representing the two panels you will cut. Since both panels will

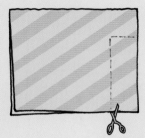

be the same size, if you have enough fabric, you can fold it in half lengthwise and cut through two layers at once.

Step 4: Hem the panels

You need to hem the ends of the panels so they look nice and finished once you sew them into the shirt. Fold the end of one of your panels over ½ inch so the party side (the pretty side) of the

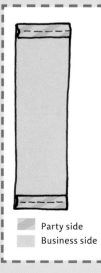

Party side
Business side

fabric is on the outside of the fold.

You can either sew the hems by hand or with a sewing machine. If you want to sew by hand, get your hand needle and an arm's length of thread. Use a running stitch, starting at one end of the folded edge. Sew a line of running stitches about ¼ inch from the edge and

finish by making several slip knots (see step 6 on page 11).

If machine sewing, use a straight stitch with a shorter length. Start on one end of the folded edge and make a straight line of stitches ¼ inch from the edge. Don't forget to backtack.

Hem the other end of the panel and both ends of the remaining panel in the same way.

Step 5: Rip the seams

Now you need to open up the seams of the shirt so you can sew in the panels. Use your seam ripper for this, starting wherever you'd like. You'll want to remove all the stitches from under the armpit and down the side of the shirt.

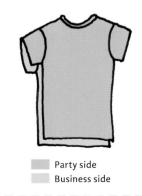
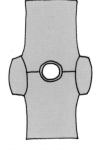

Party side
Business side

Shirt with side seams ripped open, laid flat.

Pull out the last dangly thread scraps when you're done. When you're finished, your shirt will only be attached at the neckline, across the top of the shoulders, and down the outside of the sleeves. Although it may be tempting, don't take the shortcut of cutting the shirt with scissors instead of ripping out the seams. You've made measurements with these existing seam allowances in mind.

Step 6: Pin the panels to the shirt

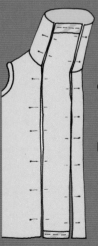

It's time to pin the panels to the ripped seams of your shirt. Start at the end of one of the sleeves and match up the hemmed corner of one of the panels to the beginning of the ripped seam. Face the party side of the panel to the outside of the shirt. Remember that when we sew these seams, we will be sewing on the business side, so it looks nice on the party side when it is turned right-side out. Place your pins ½ inch from the edge. Continue pinning down one of the long sides of the panel until

you reach the bottom of the shirt, pinning every 4 inches or so. Pin the other side of this panel, then pin the other panel to the other side of the shirt in the same way.

Step 7: Sew it all together

You can sew this by hand if you wish, but using a sewing machine will speed things up. If you want to sew by hand, get your hand needle and an

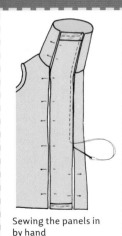

Sewing the panels in by hand

arm's length of thread. Using a running stitch, sew along the pinned lines. You can either sew right in line with the pins, removing them as you go, or just to the side of them, taking the pins out when you're done. This is a lot of stitching, and you will most likely need to rethread your needle a couple times. When you're getting close to the end of your thread, secure your stitches by making several slip knots (see step 6 on page 11) and start over with another arm's length of thread.

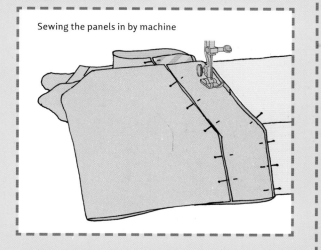

Sewing the panels in by machine

If you want to use a sewing machine, use a zigzag stitch with a medium width and length. Sew along the pinned lines, removing the pins as you go. Don't sew over the top of the pins (be nice to your machine and it will be nice to you!) and be sure to backtack.

Step 8: The finale

Once all the seams are sewn, trim off any threads and turn your shirt right-side out. If you've done everything correctly, you should be holding something that looks just like your old shirt, but better fitting and more you! Try it on, wear it out, and make sure to brag to your friends.

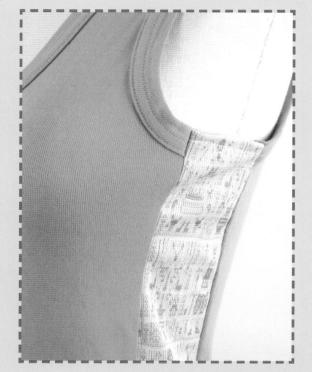

UN-TAPERFY YOUR PANTS

Tapered pants are the devil's work, we are convinced of it. We know, we all used to peg our pants when it was hip in the 1980s, but we've seen the light and had a change of heart—unless you have big ankles and no buns, stick with bootleg pants, which have a little flare in the ankle. They are more flattering and, quite frankly, a lot more fun.

What you'll need
pants or jeans
chalk
scrap of fabric (no larger than ¼ yard)
scissors
seam ripper
straight (or safety) pins
tape measure
iron and ironing board
thread that matches your pants
hand needle or sewing machine

Techniques you'll use
running stitch, if hand sewing
straight stitch and backtacking, if machine sewing

Time to complete
hand sewing: 1 hour
machine sewing: 40 minutes

When un-taperfying, don't limit yourself. You can also play around with the length of your pants and make a stylish pair of gauchos.

Step 1: Decide where to start the flare

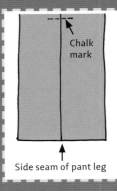

Chalk mark

Side seam of pant leg

The basics of this modification are simple: You'll just add a triangle of fabric to the ankle of your pants. First, decide where to add the extra flare. We recommend anywhere between right below the knee to midcalf. (Above the knee will look very bell-bottomy, but if that's what you're going for, rock on!) Put your pants on and mark this point on the outside seam with chalk. (You only need to mark one leg.)

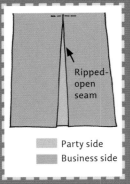

Ripped-open seam

Party side
Business side

Step 2: Rip the seams

Using your seam ripper, remove the seams from the ankle up to the mark you just made. Remove all the loose threads to keep the edges clean. Rip the second leg's seam up to the same spot and remove the loose threads.

Step 3: Cut your shape

Think about how much fabric you'd like to add to your pants (the width of the triangle). That width is basically the length of material you'll be adding to the ankle of your pants. We decided we wanted the base of our triangle to be about 5 inches (this measurement does not need to be precise). The other two legs of the triangle will correspond to how far up you ripped the seam, in our case 7 inches. Add 1 inch to each of these numbers for seam allowance. In our example, this means we need to cut out from our scrap material two isosceles triangles (geometry flashback: an

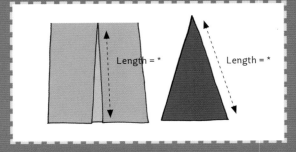

Length = *   Length = *

The length of the two equal sides of your triangle needs to equal how far you ripped up the seam of your pant leg.

isosceles triangle has two sides of the same length), with two sides measuring 8 inches long and one side 6 inches long.

Step 4: Ironin' and pinnin'

Fold ½ inch over on each edge of the triangle and iron it down. Pin the folded edges of the triangle to the edges on the seam. Make sure the party side of the triangle faces out and the top of the triangle sits slightly above the top of the point.

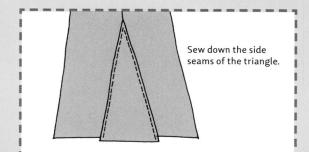

Sew down the side seams of the triangle.

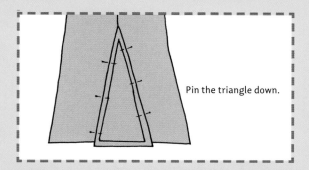

Pin the triangle down.

Step 5: Sewin' and hemmin'

Sew the triangle patch onto the jeans on each side. If you're sewing by hand, use a running stitch, and if you're using a machine, set it to a straight stitch with a short to medium stitch length. Don't forget to backtack.

Using the same stitches, hem the bottom of the triangle so it is even with the bottom edge of your pants.

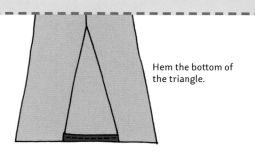

Hem the bottom of the triangle.

Tapered pants begone! We shall never have to gaze upon you again!

REFASHIONING
The Next Life of Your Old Clothes

Now we kick it up a notch. In this chapter, you'll learn how to subvert your fashion by giving new life to old clothes, what we call refashioning. Here's your chance to take pieces you kinda like and change them to create new garments you love. It's the ultimate recycling!

The first time you try these projects, you should start with a garment you like, but that is not your favorite. While you can make some amazing clothes, these projects don't necessarily have a 100 percent success rate. Part of sewing is messing up.

Some of these projects can be sewn by hand; for others, you'll need a machine. A few require no sewing at all! All of them, however, will transform that boring old garment into a very hip and very stylish new article of clothing.

TIE ONE ON IN THIS SKIRT

All you need for this project is a T-shirt. Not a cute baby-doll tee or one that fits really well—you'll want a T-shirt that's big, boxy, and not very flattering. Think about something you got for free at a street fair, or one of your boyfriend's tees (you may want to ask him before you start cutting it, though). Pick a shirt that has a great logo or silk-screened design. Since you'll be making a skirt from this T-shirt, white may not be the most modest choice, but that's your call.

You could also use a sweatshirt for this project, though it will be thicker (read: warmer and less see-through). Make sure you use a pullover, though; a zipper hoodie isn't going to work.

What you'll need

T-shirt
straight or safety pins
chalk
scissors

Techniques you'll use

cutting (that's it!)

Time to complete

10 minutes

Step 1: Prep

Find a flat worksurface (like a kitchen table or hardwood floor) and lay out your T-shirt, design-side up. Pin the front of the shirt to the back of the shirt in a few places. With your chalk, mark off lines 1½ inches to 2 inches to the inside of the sleeve seams. Mark off another line across the width of the shirt, just below the armpits, to connect the ends of the first two lines.

Step 2: Cut

Cut along the lines you just drew, removing a square piece from the top middle of the shirt, including the collar.

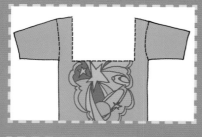

Now cut along the outside of the sleeve seams, cutting the sleeves completely off. You should have what looks like a weird tank top at this point.

Finally, cut the top of each strip (where the sleeves of the weird tank top would be) so that you have four strips of fabric attached to the top of the square piece. That square piece is your new skirt!

If you're using a sweat-shirt, make sure to cut off the waistband as well. You wouldn't want the bottom of your skirt to be tight around your legs.

Step 3: Tie

Take out the pins and step into your new (and ultra-easy-to-make) skirt. Tie each set of strips in bows or knots so that your skirt won't slip off. You can wear the ties on the sides or twist the skirt to off-center them a bit. If the fabric's a little thin, you can wear your new skirt over a vintage slip or a pair of tight jeans.

MAKE IT YOUR WAY

★ If the skirt is way too big for your hips, you can take it in a bit with your sewing machine or by hand. Just turn it inside out and stitch straight lines inside the existing seam of the shirt. You'll probably want to cut away the excess fabric when you're done.

★ If the skirt is too long, make a mark at the length you want it be, take it off, and cut it.

The skirt you made has a lot of rough edges. We did this on purpose because we like that look. If you want a more finished look, you can hem the cut edges with a machine or by hand. See page 13 for hemming info.

TOTALLY TUBE-YOU-LAR

Here's another opportunity to give new life to an old T-shirt that you just can't bring yourself to get rid of. It's also a good project for a favorite tee that has some stains or holes. The tube top you're about to make will look cute on any body style and looks ultra sexy over a pregnant belly. The T-shirt you choose can either fit you as is or be too big: We'll show you how to make it fit just right. We're going to use a technique called ruching, so you'll also need some elastic. Find yourself a fun T-shirt and let's get started! (You could also use a pullover—not a zip-up—sweatshirt for this project. The thicker fabric may come in handy since undergarments with tube tops can be tricky.)

What you'll need

T-shirt
tape measure
1 yard of ¼-inch elastic
chalk
straightedge or ruler
straight (or safety) pins
thread (to match your T-shirt)
hand needle and/or sewing machine
scissors
iron and ironing board (optional)

Techniques you'll use

running stitch, if hand sewing
zigzag stitch and backtacking, if machine sewing

Time to complete

hand sewing: 40 minutes
machine sewing: 20 minutes

Step 1: Plan it out

Lay out your shirt to decide how to orient the logo or design. Do you want it in the center of your chest? Consider it upside down, diagonal, or

on your waist—get creative! For our tube top, we wanted the design to be smack dab in the middle of the chest, right side up.

Step 2: Measure yourself

Measure your bust. Divide the number you get by 2, then add 1. So, if the widest part of your chest is 35 inches around, divide that by 2 (17½ inches) and add 1 inch for seam allowance (18½ inches). This new number is the width of the front and back panels of your tube.

Now measure on your body from where you want the shirt to start (neckline or above your bust) to where you would like it to end (waistline, or belly button, or wherever) and add 1 inch for hem allowance. In our example, we wanted the shirt to be 14½ inches long, so we cut each piece to be 15½ inches long. When deciding how long you want your tube top to be, don't forget to think about how it will rise when you reach your arms up in the air. A common mistake is to measure the length too short. Unless you are

super-duper into crop tops, err on the side of a little longer. *Hint*: If you already have a tube top made out of a similar material, use it as a guide for length and width.

Step 3: Cut it up

Front panel

Back panel

If you're using a sweatshirt, you may want to cut off the waistband, but it's not necessary. Using your chalk and straightedge, mark out the front and back panels as you measured them in step 2. Make sure that you mark the front panel so the design is where you want it. Cut both panels out.

Step 4: Get loose!

For this particular tube top, we wanted a loose fit, so we cut a slit up the back panel. Leave about 7 inches uncut at the top of the panel. (This step isn't necessary if you want a more fitted tube top.) Here's what our cut pieces look like:

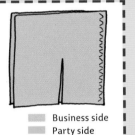

Business side
Party side

Step 5: Sew them together

Let's start sewing! Face the party sides of your panels to each other, making a party-side sandwich, and sew down one side seam. Use a running stitch if you are sewing by hand or a zigzag stitch with a medium stitch length and width on your sewing machine—don't forget to backtack! Sew this seam ½ inch from the edge of the fabric.

Step 6: Finish the top

Fold down the top ½ inch of your torso piece and pin it down to the rest of the piece. Fold it so the cut edge is on the inside of your finished shirt. It is helpful to iron this fold so it stays flat and straight, or you can use your pins to hold it

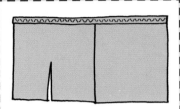

steady. Sew this edge down, using the running stitch if you're hand-sewing and the zigzag stitch if you're on a machine. This will give the shirt a finished look around the top.

Step 7: Sew it shut

Fold the piece in half, party sides together, and sew the other side seam.

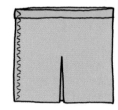

Step 8: Finish the bottom

Finish off the bottom of your shirt by folding the bottom edge under ½ inch and stitching (just like you did on the top, with the same stitches), or leave the bottom edge raw for a deconstructed look. Remember, this is your design—you can do whatever you want! You could even cut fringe along the bottom if you like.

Step 9: Ruching

We need to add some elastic to the top of the

shirt so it won't slip off when you're wearing it. Ruching is a technique that uses elastic to gather the fabric and allow for some stretch. We only ruched the front side of our shirt, but you could ruche all the way around if you really like the gathered look.

Cut a piece of ¼-inch-wide elastic to the same length as the width of your shirt (in our example, we cut an 18½-inch piece). Turn your shirt inside out and sew one end of the elastic just below the stitch line at one of the side seams to tack it in place. You can tack this down by hand or use a short straight stitch on a machine. To tack with the sewing machine, press the reverse button several times while you're sewing, so that you sew in the same spot repeatedly.

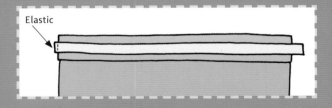

Using a running stitch, hand sew the elastic along the line just below the top edge, pulling the elastic taut as you go. This is a little tricky, but you can do it, just go slowly. Stretch the elastic, then make a stitch, stretch the elastic, then make another stitch, and so on, until you reach the other end.

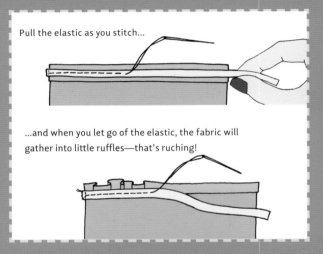

Pull the elastic as you stitch...

...and when you let go of the elastic, the fabric will gather into little ruffles—that's ruching!

You will have extra elastic when you get to end of the front panel, so cut it off after you make several slip knots (see step 6 page 11). You do not want all this work to come undone! When you turn the shirt right-side out, the top of the front side will look gathered, it will stretch, and it will stay put on your chest when you wear it.

TIPS FOR RUCHING

★ Once you have the elastic tacked to one end of the panel, you can safety-pin the tacked end to something stationary, like the jeans you are wearing or a firm sofa cushion. This will allow you to pull on the elastic without having to use your hands.

★ For a more feminine look, try ruching vertically in the middle of the bust area of your shirt, in the center of your décolletage. This added ruching is a nice way to make your tube top more form fitting. (And we all like to show off our girls!)

★ Ruching is a lot faster with a sewing machine, if you have one. Be sure to experiment on some scrap fabric before you try it on your shirt, though. Use the same technique of stretching and sewing with your machine set to a straight or zigzag stitch with a medium stitch length and width.

TOTE THAT TEE

You've got a great T-shirt or sweatshirt—a big one—you love so much that you wish you could wear it every day (except that's kinda gross). We've got the perfect solution! Turn it into a bag that you can tote along with you and maintain that whole socially acceptable "clean clothes" thing. This is much like the tube top design, except here you'll sew up the bottom and add some straps. You can also try doing this with a pillowcase.

What you'll need
sweatshirt or T-shirt
chalk
straightedge or ruler
tape measure
straight (or safety) pins
thread (to match your T-shirt)
scissors
sewing machine
iron and ironing board (optional)

Techniques you'll use
straight stitch
backtacking

Time to complete
1 hour

Step 1: Plan it
Lay out your shirt to decide how to orient the logo or design for your bag. While you can definitely put it front and center, we like it when it's a little askew. Also think about how big you

want your tote. We wanted ours to be about 12 inches wide and 6 inches tall. (Since you won't be wearing your tote, precise inches are not quite as important as they are when making garments or lined bags.) Add an inch to your desired width for a seam allowance and mark it up. We now have approximately a 13-inch by 7-inch rectangle lined up on our shirt.

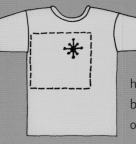

Repeat for the back side of your bag using the back of your shirt. (Or you can use another shirt. Or use the back as the front, and the front as the back. It's totally up to you.)

You will also need to cut out straps. For these, you can use what's left of the same shirt, or a ribbon, or random scraps—whatever suits you. Decide how long you want your straps to be by draping a tape measure over your shoulder to where you would want the tote to sit. Add an inch for the seam allowance. We decided on 2 feet (so it hangs down 1 foot from the shoulder) plus 1 inch for seam allowance.

How wide you want your straps to be? An inch?

Two? Eight? Take that number, double it, and add 1 inch for the seam allowance. If you want the strap to be 2 inches wide, double that, and add an inch. Now you know that the strap pieces need to be 5 inches wide.

Step 2: Cut it up

If you're using a sweatshirt, cut off the waistband so you have a flat piece of fabric to work with. Cut the front, back, and strap based on the size of the tote and the straps. When cutting the shirt, make sure to place the design where you want it to lie eventually. Remember, the front and back pieces should be the same size, as should both of the straps.

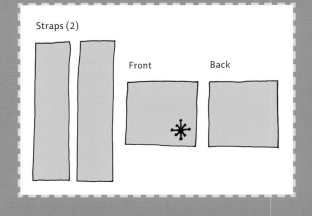

Straps (2)   Front   Back

Step 3: Let's get our sew on!

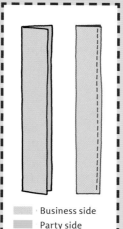

Business side
Party side

Take your first strap piece and fold it in half lengthwise (like a long taco shell), with the party sides facing each other on the inside of the taco. Now, sew a seam, using a straight stitch with a medium stitch length, ½ inch in from the cut edge, creating a long tube. Be sure to backtack.

Turn the tube right-side out. To make your strap lie flat, sew a straight stitch ½ inch in from each edge, starting from the top and stitching all the way to the bottom. (Hint: You can iron the strap flat after you turn it inside out, which may make the sewing a little easier.) Be sure to backtack. That's your first strap—make your second one the exact same way.

Step 4: Sew the side

Face the party sides of your pieces to each other, making a party side sandwich—just like you did with the straps— and sew one side seam ½ inch in from the edge of the fabric. Be sure to backtack.

Step 5: Finish the top edge

Fold down the top ½ inch or so of your bag so the cut edge is on what will be the inside of your finished tote, and pin it down. Sew this edge down, remembering to backtack. This will give the tote a finished edge around the top.

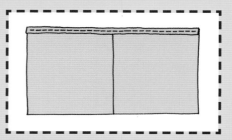

Finished strap

Step 6: Sew the other side

Fold the piece in half, matching the top sides of the bag pieces, and sew the other side seam.

With the bag inside out (party sides together), stitch the bottom closed ½ inch from the bottom. Make sure you backtack, as this is the part of the bag that carries the most stress.

Step 7: Strap it on

Pin the straps on the inside of the tote where you think they should go and try on your bag. Hey! You look great! I love your bag! We're almost done!

Step 8: Sew the straps

Sew the straps down by stitching on top of the thread line you just made to finish the top edge of the tote . Don't sew the bag together! And don't forget to backtack.

Step 9: Finish it

Finish off your tote by sewing together the bottom of the bag (a very important step if you like to actually put things in your tote).

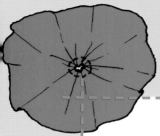

EXTRA-CREDIT EMBELLISHMENTS

★ Add anything you see fit to your tote, like big buttons or bows, or make a little flower out of your leftover fabric (see "Flower Power" below), or add a rough pocket to the front. The best time to add a pocket is after hemming the top, but before sewing the second side together. Just cut out the shape you like, pin it in place, and sew on three sides of it, leaving the top open so you can put your goods in it.

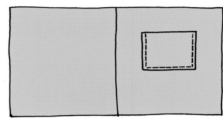

FLOWER POWER

★ To make a fabric flower out of the leftover scraps from the original T-shirt, take a long strip of fabric and sew the ends together to make a circle.

★ Then use a hand needle and thread to make a loose stitch around the bottom of this tube.

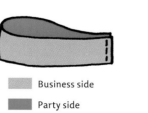

| | Business side |
| | Party side |

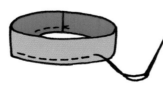

When you pull the thread taut, voilà! It's a flower!

THE HIPPEST HIP BELT IN TOWN

The pants you choose for this project should have a cute waistband and pockets —because that's all you'll be keeping. It doesn't matter one bit what the legs look like, because we're cutting them off. What you're left with is a hip-belt accessory, or a super-ultra-mini-skirt, depending on how you wear it. The pants should fit you in the waist, but make sure the waist is not so big that it won't stay up on your hips. Thicker fabric will work better for this project. You may want to choose denim or cotton, and stay away from rayon and silk. This hip belt looks great over pocketless trousers, skirts, or slips. You'll love its utilitarian value as well: pockets, pockets, pockets!

What you'll need

pants or jeans
safety pins
chalk
straightedge or ruler
scissors

Techniques you'll use

cutting

Time to com

10 minutes

Step 1: Prep

Clean off your worksurface and lay out your pants nice and flat. Pin the front of the pants to the back of the pants close to the zipper and on the sides where your hips would be. With your chalk, mark a line all the way across the width of the pants, just above the intersection of the legs and the top of the pants (aka the crotch). Start just below the zipper in the center and draw a line out to each side to make sure the line is level.

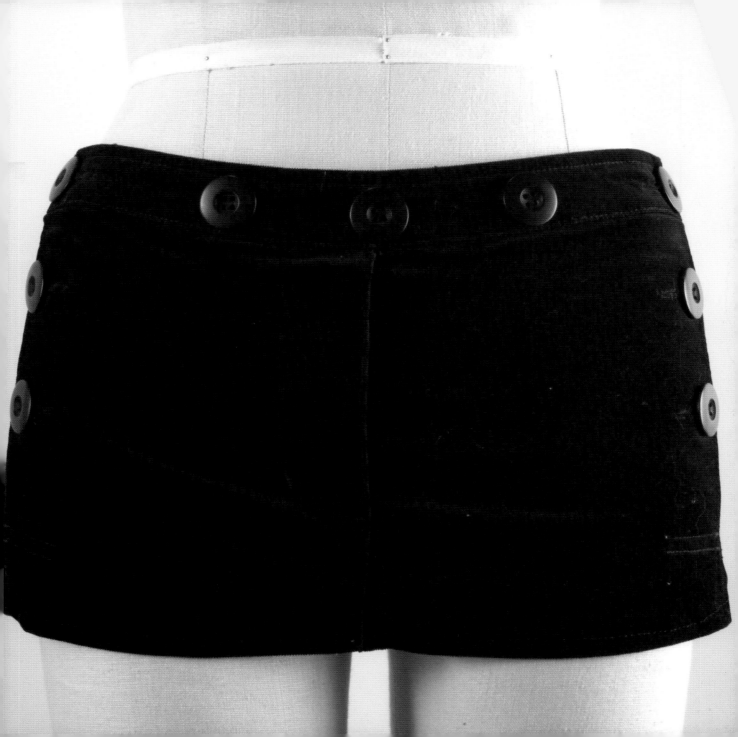

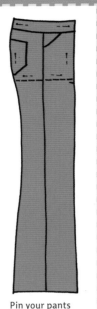

Pin your pants closed and mark your cut line.

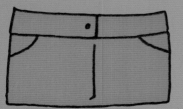

Use your straightedge if you need it, and make sure you draw the line low enough so the pockets on the back of your pants are above the line.

Step 2: Cut

Cut along the line. You're cutting off the legs and the crotch and leaving the top part of the pants. You'll be left with two pieces: one that looks like legs connected in the middle and one that looks like a hip belt or an ultra-mini-skirt. You're done! This nonsewing sewing is great!

Step 3: Fine-tune

Take out the pins and step into your new hip belt. Depending on your style, you may want to wear it over some pants or a skirt. Or you may choose to wear it as is. That's entirely up to you. You must, however, check yourself out in a mirror. Do you like the length? Is it straight? Is it even? Is it too long? You can always mark it up, take it off, and trim it as needed.

MAKE IT YOUR WAY

★ You can choose to leave the edge rough, or you can hem it up (in which case, see page 14 for a refresher on hemming). If you leave it rough and you've used denim jeans, after one or two washings you'll have a great frayed edge.

★ You can also sew some ribbon around the bottom to finish off the edge. Check out the project on page 93 for help on this technique.

GET ALL RUFFLED UP

The skirt we're about to make looks much more difficult than it actually is. All you need is an old pair of pants. Find a pair with a zipper and button or snap closure (like jeans) and preferably some pockets, though they're not required. You'll want to choose a pair that fits you well in the rear, but has legs you don't like (maybe there are holes in the knees or the legs are too short or it's got tapered legs—oh no, not again!) since we'll be cutting off most of the leg anyway. You can sew this project by hand, but it will take a lot more time, so we recommend using a sewing machine.

What you'll need

pants or jeans
fabric for ruffle (enough for a strip that's your desired width and three times the circumference of your skirt)
chalk
straightedge or ruler
scissors
seam ripper
straight (or safety) pins
tape measure
thread (either matching or contrasting with your pants)
sewing machine

Techniques you'll use

straight stitch
backtacking

Time to complete

1 hour

141

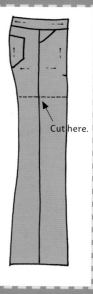

Cut here.

Step 1: Cut the length

Put the pants on, stand in front of a mirror, and, using a tape measure, decide how long you want your skirt to be. Mark off the length with chalk. You only need to mark one leg.

Take the pants off, fold them in half perfectly (check the waist and make sure both sides are lining up), and pin the two legs together. Draw a level line across the leg where you marked the skirt length. Cut along the line, through one pant leg and then the other, so that you have a pair of cutoff shorts at this point.

Party side
Business side

Step 2: Rip the seams

Using your seam ripper, remove the inside seams from the remaining portion of the legs. Remove all of the loose threads to keep the edges clean.

Step 3: Sew down the flaps

Lay out your cut-up pants nice and flat, and pin down the little flaps you now have on the front and back sides. Sew them down using a straight stitch with a medium stitch length. Don't forget to pull out the pins as you go and to backtack.

Step 4: Fill in the gaps

The front and back of the garment will have triangular gaps between the legs. We need to fill those in to complete the skirt shape. You can cut pieces from the cut-off legs of the pants or you can use some other scrap fabric (maybe the leftover pieces from the hip-belt project).

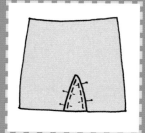

Make sure you cut the pieces slightly larger than the gaps to allow space for the seams (at least ½ inch at every seam).

Pin the cut pieces

underneath the gaps. The seams on the inside of the legs should still be intact since you used the seam ripper, so you won't have to worry about doing any extra hemming at this point (hooray!). With a straight stitch, sew in the pieces to fill the gaps. Remember to backtack and pull the pins out as you sew.

Step 5: Ruffle it up

Next, we're going to cut out the fabric for the ruffled bottom edge. You decide how wide you want your ruffle, but we're using a 1½-inch-wide strip in our example. You can cut fabric from the leftover portion of the pants or whatever you'd like to use.

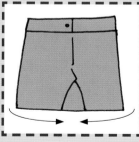

Use your tape measure to measure all the way around the bottom edge of the skirt, double that number, and you have the length of your ruffle strip.

Since you won't to be able to cut one continuous strip from the leftover fabric, cut several shorter strips, place them party side to party side, and use a straight stitch with a

½-inch seam allowance to sew them together to get one long strip that's the proper length.

Sew together the pieces for the ruffle.

For a skirt with a more finished look, add an additional inch to the desired width of the strip, then fold over one of the edges of the strip and sew it down for a hem. We're leaving our edge raw since we're using denim and it looks great frayed.

Take one end of the unhemmed side of the long strip and loosely pin it (you've got way more ruffle than skirt) to the bottom outside edge of the skirt. You are pinning the business side of the strip to the party side of the skirt because you'll be sewing the strip to the top of the skirt. Pin it so there is at least a ½-inch seam allowance. Topstitching with a straight stitch of medium length, tack down the strip where you pinned it.

Now for the magic! With a straight stitch of

medium length, start sewing the strip to the skirt. Stop after you've stitched a line about 1 to

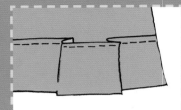

1½ inches long. Now take the strip, make a small fold at the point where you stopped stitching, and tuck that under the loose fabric, just next to the sewn spot. Continue sewing, over the tucked-in part, in a straight line, for another 1 to 1½ inches. Continue this sewing, stopping, folding, tucking thing until you have sewn a ruffle all the way around the bottom of the skirt.

Step 6: Finish it off

You may have excess strip by the time you get to the end of the ruffle. If you do, just cut it off and toss it, or use it to make another ruffle above the one you just sewed. If you used denim jeans for this project, throw your "new" skirt in the wash to fray out the edges. You're going to get lots of ooh's and ahh's on this creation, so prepare yourself!

MAKE IT YOUR WAY

★ Use a pair of sweatpants to make the cutest-ever after-workout softies. (Skirts work great for deck changing after swim practice. Bonus!)

★ Adjust the length of the skirt to your liking.

★ One is good, more is better! Add another layer of ruffles for a flirtier look. More ruffles, all the time!

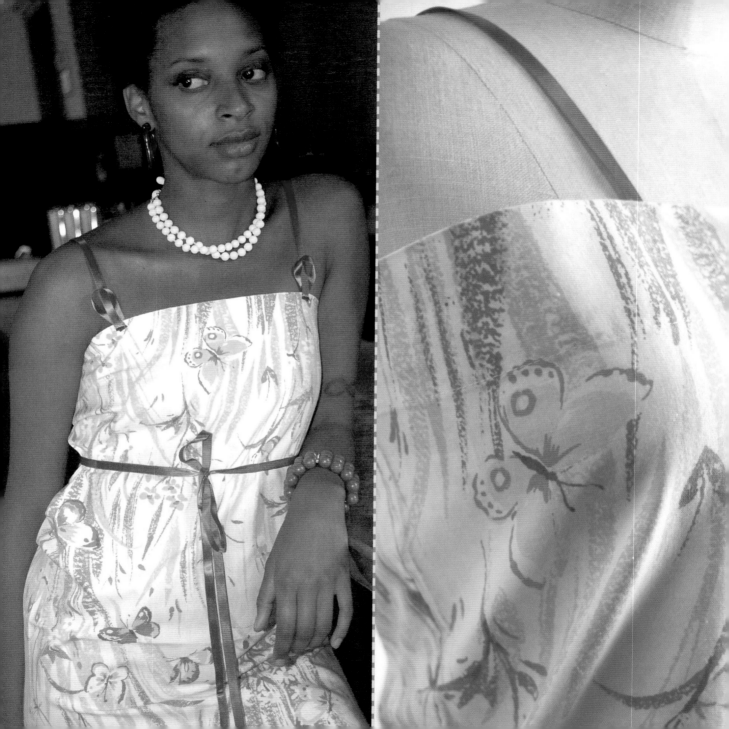

SCORE SOME PILLOW TALK IN THIS PILLOW TANK DRESS

Refashioning doesn't have to start with a piece of clothing. In this project, we transform a pillowcase into a flirty tank dress with an empire waist. Since the end product is a dress, don't pick a boring pillowcase. Find a funky pattern that you would like to wear on your body. Your grandma might have some old ones with just the pattern! If you can't find anything in the linen closet, this is another opportunity for secondhand shopping (we like to find as many opportunities for this as possible!). If it's secondhand, make sure you wash it first. Try to find a bigger pillowcase so you will fit inside it. Don't worry, though. If it doesn't fit around your hips, we'll show you how to make it work. If you have the option, get a set of two.

What you'll need

- pillowcase (set of 2 if you can)
- fabric that matches your pillowcase (in case you can't get the set of 2)
- ribbon (3 yards, no bigger than ½ inch wide)
- straight pins
- seam ripper
- straightedge or ruler
- chalk
- scissors
- tape measure
- thread (to match your pillowcase)
- hand needle or sewing machine (optional)

Techniques you'll use

running stitch, if hand sewing
straight stitch and backtacking, if machine sewing

Time to complete

hand sewing: 1 hour
machine sewing: 30 minutes

Step 1: Rip the top seam

Turn your pillowcase inside out. Using your seam ripper, take out the stitches across the top of the pillowcase so you're left with a tube.

Rip open the top seam

Pillow opening

Business side

Party side

Step 2: Measure yourself

Measure the widest part around your body; usually this is your hips (if you're lucky, this may be your bust). Divide the number you get by 2, then add 2 inches for comfort. So, if the widest part of your body is 39 inches around, divide that by 2 (19½ inches) and add 2 inches (21½ inches). This new number is the width of the front and back panels of your dress.

Step 3: Measure the pillowcase

Turn the pillowcase right-side out and lay it out nice and flat. Measure the width. The pillowcase we're using is 20 inches wide.

Step 4: Figure the difference

Compare the number you got in step 2 with the width of the pillowcase in step 3. If your width is smaller than the pillowcase, or if they are equal, you won't need to add an extra panel. You can skip to step 9.

If your dress width is larger than that of the pillowcase, like ours is, then you need to continue on in this step.

Subtract the pillowcase width from your dress width (21½ - 20 = 1½ inches, in our example), multiply this number by 2 (3 inches), and add 1 inch for the seam allowance (4 inches). This is the width of the panel (taken from that second pillowcase or other fabric) that you'll add so your dress will fit.

Step 5: Cut out the panel

If you have a second pillowcase, measure a section that is the width you calculated in step 4. Maintain the same length of the pillowcase, since all you will be doing is increasing the width of your dress. After you mark in a couple of places, draw a line to connect the dots using your straightedge and chalk. Cut out your panel.

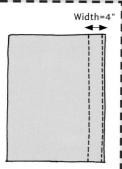

If you need to, cut out an additional panel.

If you do not have the second pillowcase of a pair, measure out a panel from your selected fabric that is the width you calculated in step 4 and the measured length of the pillow-case plus ½ inch for a hem allowance. Cut out your panel, then fold over one of the short sides ½ inch and and use a running stitch (if hand sewing) or a straight stitch with a medium length and width (if using a machine) to hem this cut end. Don't worry about the other rough edge; we'll take care of that later.

Step 6: Rip the side seam of the pillowcase

Remember, you're only doing this step if you need to add width to your dress. Turn the pillowcase inside out again and use the seam ripper to remove all of the stitches down the long side. At this point, you should be left with one big rectangle of fabric.

Step 7: Pin in the panel

Hold the party side of your panel to the party side of one of the long edges of the pillowcase. If you did not have a second pillowcase, and you cut a panel from other fabric, make sure that you line up the edge of the panel that you hemmed with

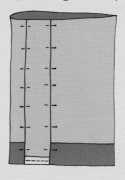

the already-hemmed edge of the pillowcase, not the rough end.

With the edges lined up neatly, place a few pins down both sides to hold it in place for sewing.

Step 8: Sew in the panel

Now let's start sewing! If you're hand sewing, use a running stitch and sew down both sides of the panel. Make sure to remove the pins as you go and to make several slip knots at the end to lock in your work. If you're machine sewing, use a straight stitch with a medium stitch length. Don't forget to backtack.

You should now have an inside-out tube that you can slip over your head and down around your body. Turn it right-side out and slip it on to see how your dress is coming along!

Step 9: Finish off the bottom edge

Turn the tube inside out. One end of your tube has rough edges and the other is already hemmed, courtesy of the original pillowcase. The already-hemmed end is going to be the top. For the bottom hem, fold over ½ inch of the rough end and place a few pins to hold it in place. Fold it so the cut edge is on the outside of the tube, which is really going to be the inside when you turn it right-side out again. Sew this edge down, with a running stitch if hand sewing, with a straight stitch with a medium stitch length if machine sewing.

Step 10: Add the straps

You first need to measure how long the straps will be. Drape the tape measure over your shoulder and hold one end at the top of your bust where you'll want the top of your dress to be. Looking in the mirror, find the spot on the tape measure where you'll want the top of the back of your dress to be (14 inches in our example). Add

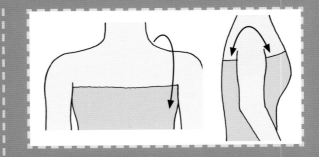

1 inch for the seam allowance (15 inches). This is how long each strap will be. We're using ribbon for the straps, so cut two pieces to the length you just determined.

Turn the tube right-side out and slip into it. Pin the front sides of the straps to the back side of the dress front where you want them to

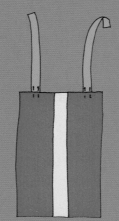

be sewn. Check this out in the mirror to be sure. You can either have a friend help you to pin the ribbons on the back, or you can pin the ribbons to the back side of the dress after you take it off. Don't overlap the ribbon by more than ½ inch on either end, since that is all we allowed for in our measurement.

Sew the ribbons where you pinned them, using a short running stitch across the width of the ribbon if hand sewing or a straight stitch on the machine.

Step 11: Your empire

Cut a piece of ribbon between 1½ and 2 yards long. This will go under the bust to cinch it in and give the dress an empire waist.

Slip on your dress. It may not look too flattering at this point. Don't worry: We're almost there.

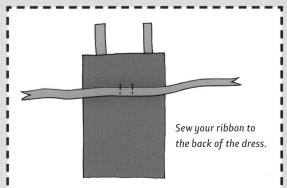

Sew your ribbon to the back of the dress.

Take the ribbon and tie it around your chest, just under your bust. Looking in the mirror, determine where it should be tacked to the dress on the back side. We chose a spot 4 inches from the top. Have a friend mark it for you with chalk or a safety pin or, if you're by yourself, just eyeball it and mark it when you take off the dress.

With the dress off, find the center point of the ribbon and sew it to the point you just marked on the dress. Using your hand needle and thread, sew a 1-inch line over the ribbon with a running stitch. Sew this over several times to make sure your ribbon will not rip off.

At this point, you're done pinning and cutting and sewing and all that stuff. Slip into your new dress, pull the ribbon around your chest, just under your bust, and tie it into a bow or knot. You just made a dress from a pillowcase! You're sew subversive!

RETURN OF THE LEG WARMERS

You can never really be sure what old-school styles will make a comeback. If you didn't know already, leg warmers are back. They are not only useful for, well, keeping your legs warm, they also look stylish with skirts, shorts, or tight pants. They can turn short boots into knee-high boots and look playful over pointy-toed shoes. This project will let you try out the look without spending any money. All you need is an old sweater that you like the look of but really don't wear anymore.

Step 1: The only thing to do is cut

All you have to do is cut the sleeves off the sweater, just before the point where they meet the body of the sweater. You want to leave the seams on the body of the sweater. It might seem ridiculously easy, but you're done!

The key to this project is putting your new leg warmers on correctly. The tight ends, where your wrists would normally go if you were wearing that old sweater, go on top, around your calf or knee. This way, the ankle portion of the leg warmer is not tapered, but instead forms a bootleg or belled look. Wear them over your shoes and let the compliments flow.

We like to leave the bottom edges rough. If you choose a sweater that is too thin, the edges may start to unravel, but you can always cut off the stray pieces or use a blanket stitch along the edge for a more finished look.

SUMMERIZE YOUR SWEATER

Find a sweater that you've grown tired of wearing in the winter, but you still dig the color or feel of. It should fit pretty well. If you choose a baggy sweater, you'll have to take it in a bit for this project (we'll talk about that, too, don't worry). Feel free to pick a crewneck, V-neck, or turtleneck sweater—just remember that this is a summer top and you may be too warm in a turtleneck halter. You could also use a T-shirt, sweatshirt, or button-down shirt for this project.

What you'll need

sweater

scissors

straight (or safety) pins

thread (to match your sweater)

hand needle or sewing machine (optional)

Techniques you'll use

running stitch, if hand sewing

zigzag stitch and backtacking, if machine sewing

Time to complete

hand sewing: 45 minutes

machine sewing: 20 minutes

Step 1: Cut it, part 1

Cut the sleeves off your sweater. Start at the armpits and cut a diagonal line toward the top of the neckline.

Try on your sleeveless sweater and make sure it isn't too baggy. It should be comfortable, but not hanging on your neck

Cut here

like it would on a wire hanger. If it is, you'll need to pare it down a bit.

Step 2: Cut it, part 2

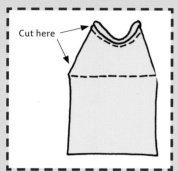

Back panel of sweater

Now we'll turn this sleeveless sweater into a halter. On the back side of the sweater, cut a straight line all the way across from one armpit to the other Finish cutting out the back panel by cutting along the bottom side of the collar. You're leaving the neckband intact.

Step 3: Finish it

All that's left to do is finish the cut edges so they won't unravel.

Fold the cut edge over ¼ to ½ inch. If you're hand sewing, use the running stitch to sew down this hem. Make small stitches so you can catch the loose knit of the sweater. You don't need to hem the neckline; it serves as its own hem.

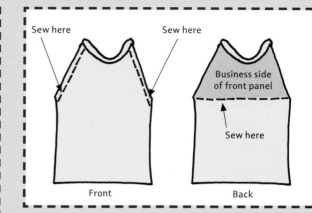

If machine sewing, sew the hem down with a zigzag stitch with a short stitch length and a narrow stitch width.

If you're using a T-shirt or button-down shirt, you can skip this step because unraveling isn't a problem. The edges won't unravel at all on a T-shirt, and a button-down

Lettuce-edge the armholes for a coquettish finish.

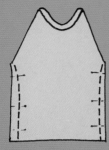

shirt made of woven fabric will fray just enough to give you a slightly frazzled look. But if you decide to do it, use a running stitch, if hand sewing, or a medium-length straight stitch on your machine.

If you used a baggy sweater, and need to form-fit it, put your sweater on inside out and pinch the fabric on each side, at the seams, so it fits the way you'd like it to. Put a couple of pins in each side to hold the pinched amount and carefully remove the sweater. (Try to make the amount of pinched fabric equal on both sides.)

Sew up these seams by hand with a running stitch, or by machine with a zigzag stitch. You'll want to make very short stitches. Depending on how much you have to take in, you may need to cut off the excess fabric after you're done sewing the new seams. But be very careful not to trim that seam too much—leave enough fabric that the sweater fabric itself doesn't unravel and create holes.

MAKE IT YOUR WAY

★ Add a twist, like Hope did with her sweater, shown here. Using a very baggy sweater, she left a piece connected to the neck in the back and got rid of the rest of the back panel. Then she sewed the front seams together (making a tube), then twisted the remaining back piece and sewed it to the top of the tube.

★ Use a T-shirt or collared shirt instead of a sweater for a different halter look.

★ Layer your halter over a long-sleeved shirt and wear it as a vest.

WINTER SWEATER, MEET WINTER HAT

We all have an old sweater in our closet that is begging to be turned into something else. Perhaps it has a hole in it; maybe it doesn't fit or is out of date. Inspired by an article in *ReadyMade* magazine, we're going to teach you how to turn it into a hat! This easy project makes a great holiday gift. Just be sure you don't give the hat to the person who gave you the sweater. (Major party foul!)

What you'll need

sweater

scissors

manila folder (to make your pattern)

thread (to match your sweater)

hand needle or sewing machine

Techniques you'll use

blanket stitch, if hand sewing

zigzag stitch and backtacking, if using a machine

Time to complete

hand sewing: 45 minutes

machine sewing: 20 minutes

Step 1: Prep the sweater

You can use either an acrylic or a wool sweater. If you have a wool sweater, it's a good idea to felt it, which we do by washing it in the washing machine on hot, then throwing it in the dryer on high. This will shrink the wool up and make it tight and a little stretchy for your hat. If you are using an acrylic/polyester sweater, it won't shrink, so you are ready to go as is.

Step 2: Decide on the shape

We've provided a couple of suggested shapes for your hat. Pick one you like, trace it onto the manila folder, and cut it out. You'll be using this to cut out the front and back of your hat. You can also use a hat you already have as a template—just lay it down flat on the folder and trace around it. Keep in mind that you'll generally want the seams on the side so you don't have a funky (or itchy) line on your forehead. To make sure the size is about right, measure around the top of your head and divide by 2. Your template should be about this wide—adjust it if it isn't. (You don't need to add a seam allowance because you'll

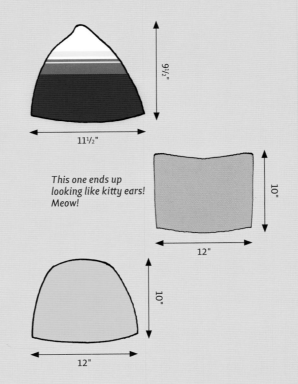

This one ends up looking like kitty ears! Meow!

want the hat to stretch a little when it's on your head. Use your best judgment on how stretchy your sweater is, but err on the smaller side. And if it winds up being too small for your head, your little cousin will surely like it! Um . . . you meant to do that, right?)

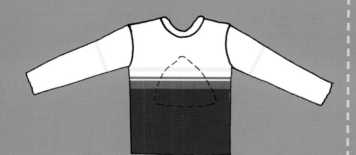

Step 3: Cut it up

Lay your manila shape on your sweater and cut out 2 pieces of the same size.

Step 4: Sew it up

Face the party pieces of the sweater together (this should be second nature to you by now) and sew around the edges by hand with a blanket stitch, leaving the part where your head will go open. The blanket stitch will wrap around the (sometimes) bulky material of the sweater and make a neat edge on the inside. You can also do this on your sewing machine with a zigzag stitch set to a medium stitch width and length. If you are concerned about your sweater fraying on the inside or on the edges, you can either do a zigzag stitch (which will make it sort of ruffly) around the outside edge or dab some FrayCheck on the edges to keep them tame.

Turn your hat right-side out, put it on, and rock out! Who's cuter than you? No one.

Once you've gotten this down, feel free to alter your pattern a little by making the back a little longer, adding earflaps, or whatever you like! We also like fabric flowers (see the directions for making them on page 135), perhaps made from another sweater, and ribbons, buttons, and patches.

SCARF SCRAPBOOK

For this project, you don't need whole sweaters, just pieces. Use your leftovers from the winter hat, halter top, and leg-warmer projects; fish out more from your closet; or hit up some garage sales, thrift stores, or even the giveaway bags of your friends and family. Find fabrics that you think look good together—gather as many as you'd like. This is a great opportunity to get rid of those really cute sweaters that just don't work for you anymore. Your new scarf will be like a scrapbook of all the sweaters you've ever loved.

You can use acrylic or wool sweaters—just remember that they will eventually be wrapped around your neck, so you don't want anything too itchy. If you're going to be using whole sweaters, you'll want at least two of them for variety. If you're using pieces, gather about one whole sweater's worth of fabric.

These scarves make great gifts. Think about refashioning the old sweaters in the back of your man's closet, the ones full of holes that are barely acceptable for public viewing. (We do advise checking with him before cutting.)

What you'll need
two whole sweaters or one sweater's worth of
    pieces
ruler or tape measure
scissors
safety pins
thread (in a color that is neutral and blends with
    all of the colors you'll be using)
hand needle or sewing machine

Step 1: Prep the sweaters

If you're using wool sweaters, it's a good idea to felt them first, which we do by washing them in the washing machine on hot, then throwing them in the dryer on high. This will shrink the wool and make it tight, a little stretchy, and much easier to cut and sew. If you are using acrylic or polyester sweaters, they won't shrink like this, so you can skip this step.

Step 2: Cut the pieces

Lay out your sweaters and cut them into strips 3 inches wide and as long as you'd like. A good overall length for the scarf is 60 inches, but, of course, yours can be longer or shorter, whatever tickles your fancy. We are going to make our scarf two strips wide, so it will be about 6 inches wide once we sew the strips together.

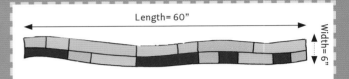

Think about how you want to design your scarf. Do you want it to be two colors, one on either side, all the way down? Do you want it to have different colors and patterns? This decision will help you plan your cutting.

From all of our sweater scraps, we cut the following pieces for our scarf:

* Four strips 3 inches wide by 15 inches long
* Four strips 3 inches wide by 10 inches long
* Eight strips 3 inches wide by 5 inches long

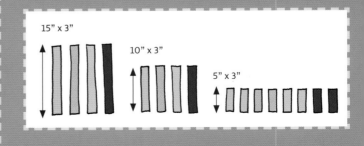

Step 3: Pin the pieces together

Lay out all of your pieces and decide how you want them to fit together. You're free to get creative; just remember that the whole thing should be a long rectangle—like a scarf. You're going to lay the edge of one piece on top of the edge of another piece, instead of face to face. (This way your scarf will look good from both sides.) Take

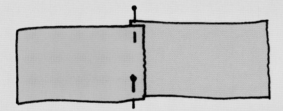

your safety pins and pin the pieces together in enough places so you don't forget your layout, but not so many that you waste your time.

Step 4: Sew it all together

If you're sewing by hand, use a running stitch and sew two lines of stitches, parallel to each other, covering the overlapped edges of the pieces. Depending on how loosely knit your sweaters are, you may need to make your stitches shorter

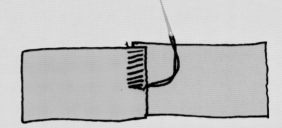

than normal; you don't want the thread to pull out of the space between the knit stitches in the sweater. This is another reason why we felt sweaters when we can.

If you're using a machine (and we suggest you do, unless you have a lot of patience), use a zigzag stitch with a short stitch length and wide stitch width. You'll be using a lot of thread here, so make sure you have a full bobbin before you begin. Use the zigzag stitches to sew together the touching edges of the pieces.

Do one final seam all the way around the whole entire scarf to help keep it from unraveling. You could do this border, or any of the seams for that matter, in a different color thread if you're into that. This is your scarf, after all!

VINTAGE NECKTIE CUFFS + COLLARS

The solution to adding some sass to any plain outfit is to accessorize. The necktie is your oyster—anything is possible! In this project, we show you an easy way to decorate your wrists. But don't stop there! Make hip belts, chokers, or sashes! You're going to need to raid your dad's, boyfriend's, friend's, or husband's closet for a necktie. By now you should know that the tie you choose should be one that he never wears, since we will be cutting it up. The good news is that if he lets you take his tie, he can wear this new wristband as well! This looks good on anyone. If the men in your life don't wear ties, are reluctant to part with them, or only own one tie (we know plenty of men like this), don't fret. Hit up a thrift store or a garage sale for a vintage tie. You're also going to need a big funky button.

Of course, you can buy one at a fabric store, but it's more fun to take one off something you already have or find when thrift-shopping. As long as the button looks good with the tie, you're good to go.

What you'll need
tie
button
tape measure
straight or safety pin
chalk
scissors
thread (to match your tie and/or button)
hand needle

Techniques
running stitch
sewing on a button

Time to complete
20 to 30 minutes

Step 1: Measure your wrist

Use your tape measure to measure around your wrist. This is easier if you have someone do it for you, but with a little dexterity, you can get it done on your own. In our example, the wrist measurement is 6 inches. Take the number you get and add 4. This will be the overall length you cut from the tie.

Length of wristband =
wrist measurement + 4 = __inches

Step 2: Cut that tie

Measuring from the pointed tip of the tie (either the wide or narrow end, your choice), make a mark with a pin at the length you just determined in step 1 (10 inches in our case). Cut a straight line across the width of the tie at the point you just marked. Don't forget to take the pin out as you are cutting.

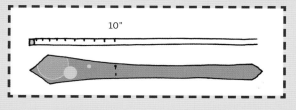

10"

Step 3: Hem the cut end

Fold the cut end of your tie over ½ inch and pin this hem down. Make sure to fold the cut end toward the business side of the tie. Now sew a running stitch across the width of the cut. Make sure to make several slip knots at the end so your stitching doesn't come loose.

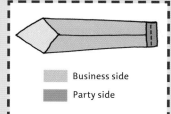

Business side
Party side

Step 4: Sew on the button

Sew the button on the end you just hemmed, placing it ½ inch from the edge and centered across the tie. Remember to insert the pin in your tie (see page 11) to create space between the button and the tie, so that you'll be able to get the buttonhole around the button when you're done.

Step 5: Cut the buttonhole

You're going to cut the buttonhole 1 to 1½ inches in from the pointed end of the tie. Mark this point with chalk, right in the center of the tie's width.

The buttonhole needs to be big enough so the button will fit through, but not so big that the button slips out while you are wearing it. Measure the diameter of your button. Ours is 1 inch. You want your buttonhole to be just a tiny bit smaller than this diameter (we're talking tiny like ⅛ inch smaller). Divide that measurement by 2 and make a mark on either side of your center point, lengthwise, to that length. Draw a line to connect your two points; this is the length of your buttonhole.

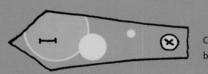

Center of buttonhole

The simplest way to cut the buttonhole is to fold the tie at the center of the line you just drew and to cut along the line. Unfold your tie, and, *voilà*, you have a buttonhole.

The buttonhole will have some rough edges, but it's not a big deal because it will hide behind the button when you are wearing your wrist cuff. If you are a perfectionist and want finished edges, use your sewing machine, with the buttonhole foot, to make a mo' fessional buttonhole. Check your sewing machine manual for instructions on this technique.

Step 5: Flaunt it

Your wrist cuff is ready to flaunt! If you like the look, try making neck collars or even belts. All that changes is the length of tie you cut.

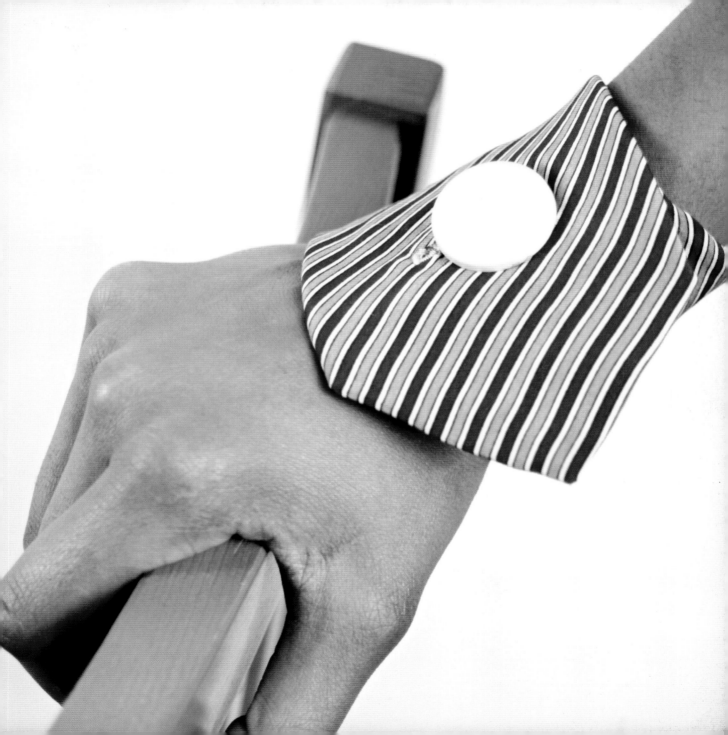

I'M A SLEEVE TO WINE!

Fabulous fashionistas not only look good, but they also have excellent style and grace. A fashionable lady knows never to show up at a friend's house for dinner or a party without a hostess gift. If you are anything like us, the gift is usually a bottle of wine or champagne. A simple trick is to keep homemade, fabulous wine bags on hand, so even a bottle of Two-Buck Chuck looks divine. Paper wine bags from the corner store are overpriced and, frankly, not that cute. We took a sweater sleeve and a man's shirt and tie and turned them into two creative and cute (and nearly free) wine bags. Grab an old shirt and let's get to it!

What you'll need

either
* ★ long-sleeved shirt
* ★ ribbon or thin cord (½ yard—this will be your drawstring)

or
* ★ man's long-sleeved shirt with button cuffs (French preferred)
* ★ man's necktie
* ★ ¼ yard of the thinnest elastic you can find

bottle of wine

scissors

thread

hand needle or sewing machine

Techniques you'll use

running stitch, if hand sewing

straight stitch and backtacking, if machine sewing

Time to complete

hand sewing: 30 minutes

machine sewing: 20 minutes

Step 1: Fit it

Stick the wine bottle in the sleeve of whichever shirt you are using (with the cork or screw top pointing out of the cuff). If you are using a long-sleeved shirt, stick the bottle in far enough so the top of the bottle is covered. If you are using the man's shirt, the cuff will act as the wine bag's "collar," so unbutton the cuff and fold it over, as if the sleeves are starting to be rolled up. You'll want the top of the bag to be the "collar" near the neck of the bottle (where the bottle starts to taper off). This is where the tie will rest. Pinch the sleeve below the bottle to close off the bag (imagine that you are estimating where the bag

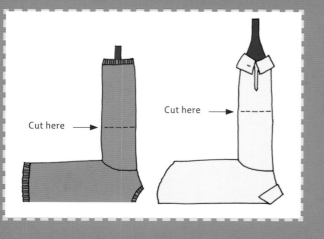

will end). Cut the sleeve off a little farther toward the shoulder than where your fingers are.

Step 2: Sew it

Turn the sleeve inside out and, with a ½-inch seam allowance, sew the bottom of the bag shut (either by hand or machine). You will not need pins for this, as it's a short distance to sew. Turn the sleeve right-side out and stick your bottle

in again to make sure you like the length (and that the bottle stands up straight— if not, trim some of the seam allow-ance off).

Step 3: Tie it

You will need to add a drawstring (or elastic tie) to the top of the sleeve/bag to make sure it stays up over the bottle. The easiest way to do this with the shirt sleeve (we'll get to the cuffed sleeve in a second) is to clip little slits (about the width of your ribbon or cord—no more than ½ inch

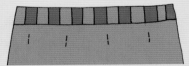

in length) 2 inches down from the top (or around where the neck of the bottle starts), all the way around the sleeve. This is where you will thread your drawstring. You should clip a minimum of 6 slits, but any even number will do. (The number needs to be even so that when you thread it, your drawstring winds up on the outside of the bag so you can tie it.)

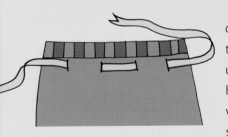

Thread your drawstring through the slits (over and under, almost like hand sewing, but without a needle), slip the bottle of wine back in, and tie the ends of the drawstring together in a bow. You can embellish the drawstring by adding a button or pin to the end of it. Or punch a hole in a piece of stationery paper, write a quick thank you to your hostess, and thread it on the drawstring. You decide. Repeat with the other sleeve of the shirt so you have a spare for last-minute gift emergencies! (Don't forget to remove the price tag from the wine!)

As for the cuffed shirt, you'll need to make a faux tie. Turn the bag right-side out and fold the cuff over as if it were the collar on the bag. Put the bottle in the bag and wrap your thin elastic under the collar, just tight enough to hold it up. Either tie a knot or sew the elastic shut. Trim off the excess. You should now have a thin elastic ring.

To create the mini tie, cut off a 6-inch to 8-inch length from the wide end of the tie, keeping the pointy end intact. (Some people like short ties, some like 'em long.) This is going to be the mini tie. If you want to use the small end of the tie,

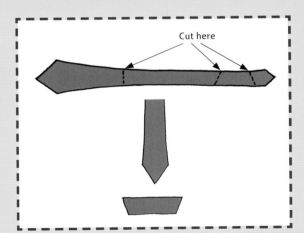

Cut here

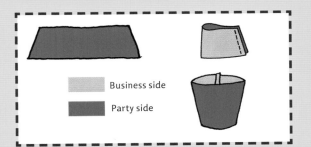

Business side

Party side

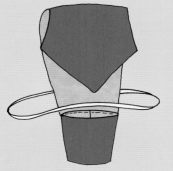

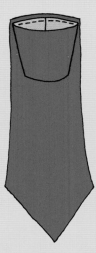

feel free, but remember that your design will be upside down on the finished tie (and you'll need to take any visible tags off). Cut a 3-inch length from the narrow end of the tie. This part will be your faux knot (think clip-on tie). Make your cuts angled so the piece is 1 inch wider on the top than the bottom (a trapezoid shape, if you will).

Take the trapezoid piece, face party side to party side, sew the short sides together with a ½-inch seam allowance, and turn it right-side out. It should look like a tie knot, but with a point on the top back part (where the opening is wider).

Face the front of the long piece you cut off to the back of the knot (the party side, where the seam is). Sew the top of the tie to the point of the knot.

You can probably see where this is going. You will then slip the long tie through the faux knot. But not so fast! First slip your elastic ring between the tie and the knot, so that when you thread the tie through the knot, it will hold in place.

Slip your gorgeous tie under the collar of your wine bag, and you've got a delightful man's shirt wine bag. Grab another tie and the other sleeve and make yourself a spare!

REFASHION YOURSELF

Now that your brain is whizzing with lots of refashioning ideas, why not throw a refashioning get-together? Drag your craftiest of crafty friends (or those who aren't so crafty who could use some inspiration, or who would at least be willing to make sure the champagne flutes are always full) and go crazy. We did just that by pulling together some of San Francisco's talented up-and-coming designers. The task was simple: Take an "I ❤ NY" T-shirt and go at it! As you can see, a simple shirt has tons of potential.

We've also participated in a Garment ReMake Exchange put on by a local artist and designer, Helena. Helena's website, www.garmentremake.com, explains the Garment ReMake as "a pen-pal system, but instead of sending letters, participants send clothes, and instead of writing, we are sewing. Each exchange takes place between two groups of people located in two different cities." Each person submits an item of clothing, then gets an item of clothing from the partnering city. Everyone refashions, then trades back to the original owner. Sometimes the groups get together and work on their garments, but however it's done, everyone comes home with something new and delicious!

See! The possibilities are endless! Now get planning . . .

What you'll need
at least one item of clothing for each person
   (people can BYO to make sure they have
   something that resonates with their taste)
sewing gear as described throughout the tutorials
   (people can also BYO sewing kits)
delightful accoutrements to share
sewing machine (optional)
enough copies of *Sew Subversive* to go around
munchies and refreshers

Techniques you'll use
(d) all of the above!

Time to complete
Plan for an afternoon or evening of good-time fun.

Step 1: Go wild!

Let your imagination run free! Turn that T-shirt into a tube top, hem those pants, or try something else you've been inspired to do. Ask your friends for ideas. Don't be afraid to mess up.

Step 2: Strut your stuff!

Make sure to allow time for you and your hot friends to go out on the town (if even just for coffee at the local beanery) and show off your new creations!

**You look great!
Our work here is done.**

RESOURCES

Garment districts
(for fabric and other fun stuff!)
Los Angeles
  http://fashiondistrict.org/
New York
  www.fashioncenter.com

Second hand stores
Goodwill
  www.goodwill.org/page/guest/about
Buffalo Exchange
  www.buffaloexchange.com
Cross Roads
Salvation Army

New clothing to play with
http://www.americanapparel.net/

Sewing machine manufacturers
Bernina
  www.berninausa.com/home.jsp
Singer
  www.singerco.com
Elna
  www.elna.com/en/index
Viking
  www.husqvarnaviking.com
Janome
  www.janome.com
Necchi
  www.necchi.it
Brother
  www.brother-usa.com/HomeSewing

White
  http://www.whitesewing.com/
Pfaff
  http://www.pfaff.com/
Kenmore
  www.sears.com/kenmore/

Notions Suppliers
Prym-Dritz
  (Stitch Witchery, Fray Check, sewing accoutrements)
Gütterman Thread

Other places we buy machines
www.craigslist.org
www.ebay.com
Estate & yard sales

Crafty & Inspirational DIY websites
www.craftster.org
www.getcrafty.com
www.ohystars.net
www.garmentremake.com
http://www.churchofcraft.org/
http://fashiondiy.blogsome.com/category/diy/
http://supernaturale.com/
http://www.thecreativelife.tv/
http://www.instructables.com
http://www.notmartha.org
http://www.diynet.com
http://www.deborahmerlo.com
http://www.teengirlclothing.com/DIY.html
http://www.allcrafts.net/sewing.htm#freeprojects
http://www.fitzpatterns.com/
http://www.livejournal.com/community/t_shirt_surgery/
http://www.livejournal.com/community/craftgrrl/
http://www.livejournal.com/community/clothes_surgery/

Other websites we like

www.styleindustry.com (resources for fashion industry)

www.patternreview.com (reviews on different brands and makes of sewing machines)

On-line sewing supplies

www.Sewtrue.com

Repro Depot Fabrics
(Great vintage reproduction and retro themed fabrics)

http://www.reprodepotfabrics.com/

National in-store sewing supplies

Joann Fabrics
www.joanns.com

Michaels Arts and Crafts
http://www.michaels.com/

Hancock Fabrics

Magazines

Readymade
www.readymademag.com

Bust
http://www.bust.com/

Sewing Lounges

Stitch Lounge, Inc (San Francisco)
www.stitchlounge.com

Stitches (Seattle)
www.stitchesseattle.com

Make Workshop (New York)
www.makeworkshop.com

First Samples (Austin)
http://www.firstsamples.com/index.shtml

The Sewing Lounge (MN)
http://www.textilecentermn.org

SF Bay Area Fabric Stores

Discount Fabrics
525 4th Street, San Francisco, CA 94107
(415) 495-4201
2315 Irving Street, San Francisco, CA 94122
(415) 564-7333
1432 Haight Street, San Francisco, CA 94117
(415) 621-5584
3006 San Pablo Avenue, Berkeley, CA 94702
(510) 548-2981

Fabric Outlet
2109 Mission Street, San Francisco, CA 94110
(415) 552-4525

Mendel's Far Out Fabrics & Art Supplies
1556 Haight Street, San Francisco, CA 94117
(415) 621-1287

Darlene's Fabrics
2877 Mission Street, San Francisco, CA 94110
(415) 550-0149

Britex Fabrics
117 Post Street, San Francisco, CA 94108
(415) 392-2910

Stone Mountain & Daughter Fine Fabrics
2518 Shattuck Avenue, Berkeley, CA 94704
(510) 845-6106

Poppy Fabric
5151 Broadway, Oakland, CA 94611
(510) 655-5151

Jo-Ann Fabrics & Crafts
75 Colma Boulevard, Colma, CA 94014
(650) 755-1711

INDEX